MENTAL DISCIPLINE

HOW TO BUILD SELF-DISCIPLINE AND ACHIEVE YOUR GOALS. CHANGE YOUR MIND, CONTROL YOUR THOUGHTS TO ACHIEVE SUCCESS WITH A POSITIVE MENTAL ATTITUDE AND SELF-CONTROL.

Author's name
Joe Mind

Table of Content

INTRODUCTION 5

CHAPTER 1. THE SCIENCE AND PSYCHOLOGY OF SELF-DISCIPLINE 9

   BENEFITS AND DRAWBACKS OF STRENGTHENING SELF-DISCIPLINE BENEFITS OF HAVING SELF-DISCIPLINE 9
   THE DIFFERENCE BETWEEN CONVENTIONAL DISCIPLINE AND SELF-DISCIPLINE 14
   WHAT IS SELF-DISCIPLINE? 19

CHAPTER 2. SELF-DISCIPLINE AND FREEDOM 22

   WHY SELF-DISCIPLINE IS THE KEY TO SUCCESS 22
   WHY SACRIFICE IS A KEY TO YOUR SUCCESS 27
   CAUSES OF LOW SELF-DISCIPLINE 27
   YOUR BEHAVIOR AND ITS MOST BASIC FOUNDATIONS 32

CHAPTER 3. HOW TO DEVELOP SELF DISCIPLINE 38

   INVEST IN SELF-REGULATION 38
   COGNITION AND ITS ROLE IN SELF-DISCIPLINE 39
   TRAITS OF SELF-DISCIPLINED PEOPLE 41

CHAPTER 4. DAILY SELF-DISCIPLINE 54

   IMPROVING CONCENTRATION 54
   BUILDING MENTAL TOUGHNESS 56
   CONTROL YOUR MIND 57
   BUILDING ON YOUR GOOD HABITS AND GETTING RID OF NEGATIVE ONES 59
   BUILD UP YOUR DAILY ROUTINE 62
   FORMING GOOD HABITS AND BREAKING BAD HABITS 63
   TRACK YOUR PROGRESS 67

CHAPTER 5. IMPORTANT TECHNIQUES 70

   TECHNIQUES THAT ENSURE OPTIMAL PRODUCTIVITY 70
   TECHNIQUES FOR DEVELOPING GREATER SELF-DISCIPLINE 74

CHAPTER 6. UTILIZATION AND APPLICATION OF POSITIVE HABITS 78

   THE IMPORTANCE OF IDENTIFYING BAD HABITS 78
   EXPLORING HABITS AND THEIR IMPACT ON SELF-CONTROL 79
   HABITS TO BECOME MORE PRODUCTIVE 85

CHAPTER 7. MENTAL TOUGHNESS AND PERSONAL GOALS 93
- How To Build Mental Toughness 93
- Your Personal Goals 97
- Your Overall Happiness 99

CHAPTER 8. UNDERSTANDING THE DIFFERENCE BETWEEN MENTAL TOUGHNESS AND RESILIENCE 109

CHAPTER 9. THE PITFALLS OF IMPROVING SELF-DISCIPLINE 126

CHAPTER 10. THE DIFFERENCE BETWEEN SELF-DISCIPLINE AND SELF-CONTROL 134

CHAPTER 11. SELF-DISCIPLINE, CONFIDENCE AND MOTIVATION 145

CHAPTER 12. TECHNIQUES TO IMPROVE YOUR MENTAL TOUGHNESS 162
- Improving Focus With The Help Of Meditation And Visualization 162
- Enhancing Visualization To Improve Focus 163
- Giving Your Best When Under Pressure 165
- Staying Motivated 165
- Developing Self-Control 167
- Taking On Challenges And Responsibilities 168
- Embracing Positive Thinking 169
- Determination To Succeed 170
- Distinguishing Between The Controllable And Uncontrollable .. 171
- Accepting That Competition Is Inevitable 172
- Bouncing Back From Setbacks 172
- Developing Unshakable Self-Belief In Your Abilities To Succeed 173
- Acquiring The Necessary Skills Required To Accomplish Your Goal 174
- Developing Your Cognitive Mind To Think Like A Winner 174
- Developing Resilience 175
- Commitment To Achieving Your Goals 176
- Surrounding Yourself With Positive People 177

CHAPTER 13. MORE THAN MOTIVATED: MINDSET CHANGES YOU NEED TO MAKE 180

CONCLUSION 187

Introduction

This volume is intended to be an in-depth guide to developing self-discipline. It is not just a pleasant read to be read once and set on the coffee table to use for looks. This manuscript is meant to be an in-depth guide toward knowing and implementing all the steps needed to achieve self-discipline.

Read through the volume once, and then read through it again. The first read is merely to become familiar with what self-discipline really is. The second read should be slower and more in-depth to allow the reader time to process the tips and tricks included here and to imagine how these changes will fit into their current lifestyle. More importantly, this will allow time to begin to visualize these changes as a part of the everyday lifestyle and how the changes will fit.

Some of the ideas contained in this volume will make more sense when they are actually used. Let's say that one goal is to save more money. Work out a plan to save—a personal plan. If cash is still the basis of most daily transactions, then put a dollar a day into a jar on the dresser. Take the spare pocket change and dump it in the jar every night. Many financial institutions offer ways to take money from the checking account, based on transactions, and transfer it to the savings account.

A payroll deduction to a savings account might work. Whatever the method, the first most important step is to set the goal and the method that will be used to achieve the goal. Now, sit back and watch that money grow. Watch that jar on the dresser get a bit fuller every week. Watch how the amount in the savings account keeps increasing. This is how goals are achieved. It is not enough to want to save money. It is necessary to make the goal to save money as well as the plan to save money and then watch it grow.

Do not be afraid to try and fail. No one succeeds completely with the first attempt. Actually, that is a good thing. If self-discipline were that easy to achieve, then everyone would have it and possessing it would no longer be so special. Besides, trial and error are an important part of personal growth. The important thing is to begin, to try. Talking about beginning will not work. It is a good thing to spend some time considering this new journey, but the person who waits for some far-off ideal moment will never begin. "Tomorrow," "someday," and "eventually" no longer have a spot in the vocabulary of the person who desires self-discipline. The time is now.

Keep sight of the ultimate goal. Do whatever is needed to keep that goal fresh in the mind. Draw a picture and hang it on the refrigerator. Keep a detailed journal of daily events that will lead to the achievement of the goal. Tell family and friends about the goal. The more it is out front and visible, the harder it is to ignore—and by not keeping it a secret, the chances of failure are decreased. No one wants to fail in public!

By using the ideas contained in this volume and really putting effort into it, anyone can become more self-disciplined. It will not happen overnight—but with hard work and concentration, it will happen.

Chapter 1. The Science and Psychology of Self-Discipline

Benefits And Drawbacks Of Strengthening Self-Discipline Benefits Of Having Self-Discipline

When a person has strong self-discipline, it leads to higher self-regard, inner strength, self-assurance, and ultimately, satisfaction and happiness. It leads to better outcomes in every area of a person's life. The following benefits of self-discipline are ones that may not automatically come to mind.

Benefit #1: Self-Discipline Creates Inner Strength and Character

According to a famous psychology volume, there was an important statement that the author wrote. He stated that everyone is the person that they wish to be. All that is stopping you from behaving in the manner that you want to behave is your emotional mind. Let's think about that for a second. Although you may be a very kind and caring person, if you tend to lose your temper easily, other people may see you as a hothead or an angry person. In this example, you don't necessarily need to change who you are as a person. Instead, you need to change the way you behave. Once you change the way you behave, other people will then see you for the person that you truly are. For example, you already are that kind and caring person, but your short temper is preventing you from showing that personality to the world. Your self-discipline is a tool that can help you to stop acting on your impulses and instead act based on your true character.

Benefit #2: Self-Discipline Allows You to Resist Temptations

As we conferred in part, our modern-day lives are filled to the brim with temptations that can throw people off track and prevent them from achieving their goals. Often, these temptations are temporary, and by exercising willpower, most people can overcome the urge. In our modern workplace, temptations tend to take the form of distractions like checking your phone, a conversation at the water cooler, or scrolling through social media. Those examples are just the tip of the iceberg when it comes to our potential modern-day distractions. When you can recognize what your temptations are, you can place a strategy in order to prevent caving to it. This requires less self-discipline compared to ignoring the temptation with brute mental force. For example, if your coworker locks her phone in the drawer of her desk and refuses to check her phone during the workday. She may make this strategy easier for her by telling all her friends that she does this so that her friends do not expect an immediate response. As we already learned, temptations also exist in the form of addictions and bad habits. When self-disciplined is coupled with effective strategies, it is a very valuable tool that can be used to overcome most urges in life.

Benefit #3: Stronger Self-Discipline Increases One's Chances of Success

When a goal can be achieved with great ease, some would argue whether it should even be considered a goal or not. Goals require a person to stretch and grow; to improve skills, attitudes, and to improve one's knowledge. When an individual meets those requirements, they improve the quality of their life along with improving their capability to take on larger and harder challenges. Ultimately, goals should be challenging. Everyone will face barriers and obstacles in which they would need to overcome. This is the action that is needed in order to create personal growth. In order to overcome these obstacles and barriers to achieve your goals. It will require a lot of self-discipline and self-belief. A person's ability to persevere and overcome obstacles when faced with difficulty is often the difference between failure and success.

Benefit #4: People with Self-Discipline Build Better Relationships

Take a minute to think about some of the things that you value in a relationship. This could be a friendship, a romantic relationship, or a familial relationship. You may value important things like integrity, dependability, loyalty, and honesty. All these traits require a person to have a strong character. It requires someone who can be true and act true to their values and beliefs, even when it would be easier to fall into temptation. As we already conversed, those with self-discipline are more likely to develop a stronger character. They have a lot of practice in doing the things that they know need to be done, even though they would probably rather be doing something else. Generally, they are a person that most people can count on. They are more effective when it comes to gaining respect and building trust amongst their peers.

Benefit #5: Self-Discipline Makes It More Difficult for a Person to Be Offended

People with more self-discipline tend to be calmer, assured, and more confident. They know who they are as a person and what they believe in. They will always do what they believe to be the right thing. As we mentioned throughout this volume, although the task that needs to be done may not be something that they want to do at that very moment in time, the strength of self-discipline demands them to be true to their values and beliefs. One of the major benefits of this behavior of a self-disciplined person is that they can always be confident that they have done their best. If a person knows that they tried their very best and couldn't have done any better, they will be able to hold their heads up high, knowing that any insults or criticism are meaningless. However, this person would also be prepared to listen to any constructive criticism, but negative feedback does not affect them much at all. To maximize the benefits of self-discipline, a person must have goals that are effective in motivating and inspiring them.

The Difference Between Conventional Discipline And Self-Discipline

Self-Discipline

Self-discipline is a skillset and also a lifestyle—you can have self-discipline skills but not necessarily be self-disciplined if you fail to use them on a regular basis. Not only must you learn the skills necessary, but you must also make sure that you are able to live that lifestyle as well. The entire purpose of self-discipline is to make the right decision, no matter whether it means you do not get that instant gratification that you were craving. When you are self-disciplined, you are able to get past that. You can see that brownie sitting on the corner and remind yourself that you have already had your treat for the day and that the brownie is out of the question, and then move on with your life as if nothing has happened.

Self-discipline can appear in many different forms that you may not realize. It can be perseverance—despite the challenge that you are facing, you can choose to keep going and keep trying, despite the exhaustion and despite the lack of motivation, you have to continue. It can be restraint—you can tell yourself that you will not be making a choice that may be enjoyable short-term, but you know will not be worth it long-term. It can be following your plan to a T instead of floundering between doing and not doing whatever your plan was until you are out of time anyway. It can be pushing past the hardships that whatever is required will cause and finishing the job, no matter what the cost or effort necessary.

Self-Discipline in Your Life

When you are self-disciplined, you are controlled. You are able to avoid negative consequences simply by knowing how to resist the temptation you feel that tries to convince you to do something. It is not the restrictive life of rejecting everything enjoyable that you may be thinking of—instead, it is an ability to balance your own goals and aspirations with what you really must do in order to see those results at the end of the day. You are able to enjoy yourself while not erring on the side of being lazy or greedy. Think of it as an exercise in moderation—when you are self-disciplined. You can live by that moderation without falling into the trap of eating or drinking in excess.

This lifestyle that you are living when you are self-disciplined is healthier, then. It is one with motivation, with drive, and with a clear idea of what you want to achieve and why. This is why self-discipline is so crucial, especially in today's world, where your dozens of ways in which you can satisfy yourself with instant gratification. Especially if you live in a major metro area, you may find that you have access to anything you may want within hours or days with delivery options available now. You do not have to leave the hope of buying anything—it can all be delivered straight to you. You do not have to go outside to make friends—you can do it online. You can even date online to find romantic partners without ever having to try to put in the effort to get to know the other person to see if you may be compatible—instead, you simply take a quiz, make a profile, and wait for computer algorithms to match you with other people that you may be compatible with.

In a world of being able to get anything and everything instantly without having to work for it or find it elsewhere, you have little in life that forces you to learn to be self-disciplined. Not much actually requires effort to become satisfied anymore. You do not have to hunt to survive, nor do you have to garden and forage. All you have to do is go to the store to buy something. If you have children, you can pay someone to come and take care of them for you. Essentially, these days, almost anything that required self-discipline before can be achieved with money.

Of course, you may be thinking of that old adage that money does not buy happiness, and that is exactly where self-discipline comes in. It is hard to feel satisfied and enjoyment in life when you are simply getting by with no effort. It is tough to feel like you are happy with yourself when you do not have to work to live. Life becomes boring and tedious, and you become unmotivated. Self-discipline can help you regain that motivation that you may have lost long ago and rekindled it into something powerful and helpful for you. Self-motivation can help you bring back the joy in your life that you may feel is lacking.

Mindset and Discipline

The mindset that you make in life absolutely matters. If you want to be disciplined, you need to develop the mindset for it. When you create a certain mindset, you create a frame through which you see the world. You are able to see things in the context that you have encouraged in order to keep you on the right track. Think of how a religious individual with a religious mindset may have little problem fasting as dictated by their religion, but someone without that mindset, who may have decided to fast just because may find that it is infinitely harder than the individual who is doing so for their religion.

The power of the mindset is undeniable. It determines how you see yourself. It determines the context through which you interact with the world. More importantly, it shapes how likely you are to become successful in your endeavors to be self-disciplined. By and large, there are two distinct types of mindsets: The fixed mindset and the growth mindset. Each of these serves its own purpose, but what you want to develop for yourself is the growth mindset.

The Self-Discipline Mindset

Your self-discipline mindset will have two crucial factors to it, both of which are contingent upon being within the growth mindset, to begin with. You need to first believe that you are able to make the changes you need to sculpt yourself into the person that you wish to become if you desire to develop self-discipline. Once you have accepted that your own abilities are far from static, you can move on. The two crucial factors to self-discipline are creating a mindset that is aligned with commitment and is free of self-judgment.

What Is Self-Discipline?

It takes a high degree of restraint and willpower to make beneficial decisions on a daily basis especially because we are daily faced with the choice of making several decisions. This ability enables us to resist the temptation of making comfortable decisions.

It might seem very easy to make the option of the easiest solution, but in reality, it's only temporary. Majority of these "comfortable choices" may not really contribute to your success when you reflect on it from a long-term perspective. It might look harmless when you make those pleasurable decisions continually. However, the totality of all unprofitable little decisions will determine the course of your life and destiny.

Self-Discipline is a noun which can be described in the following sentences:

- The capability to bridle your emotions and desires
- The capability to do things that need to be done
- The capability to direct and master your conduct

Self-Discipline is a noun that explains the essential mental energy to bridle an individual's emotions, actions, and desires. A self-disciplined person has his/her emotions and cravings under check. An individual with a high degree of self-discipline will not run away from challenges and difficult situations, because self-discipline also reflects that a person can handle problems and duties that come his/her way.

Chapter 2. Self-discipline and Freedom

Why Self-Discipline Is The Key To Success

Many researchers suggest that the single most important thing in a person's ability to become successful is their level of self-discipline. Self-discipline is responsible for helping people stay focused on reaching their goals, gives them the grit that they need to stick with difficult tasks, and allows them to overcome barriers and discomforts as they push themselves to achieve greater things.

People Cannot Achieve Their Goals Without Self-Discipline

People cannot achieve their goals without self-discipline, so make sure that you are supplementing your goals with a self-discipline list. It will help you focus on the tasks and behaviors that you need to perform in order to achieve the goals that you want. For example, one of my goals is to lose 10 pounds by December. My discipline list will include things like avoiding fast food, buying more fruits and vegetables, and making sure to hit the gym at least twice a week. High self-discipline, in this example, would be doing everything on that list without any exception. This does not mean that you cannot reward yourself or take a break from working towards your goals; it simply means that you should get the things done on your list before you indulge in any rewards.

Use a Daily "To-Do" List to Track the Things You Need to Get Done

Make sure you are using a daily to-do list to keep track of all the things that you need to get done in order to achieve your goals. Try to use online tools or just a simple note that can help you prioritize and organize. It feels very satisfying to be able to check off items that you've completed, and it will even motivate you to finish other tasks that are on your list just to feel the satisfaction of being able to check off another box. Make sure your to-do list works together with your discipline list to help yourself stay on track. A useful tip to keep in mind when you're feeling unmotivated is to start off with the easiest item on the list just to get the ball rolling. Once you complete one easy task, people normally feel more motivated than before; this will help you get started on the rest of your list. Starting with a harder task May create apprehension about doing it, therefore, start small and work your way up.

Figure Out Which Obstacles Are Holding You Back from Success

Different people have different things that distract them from being able to complete important tasks. For example, a person that is easily distracted by emails and people in their office might have to close their office door as soon as they get into work to get their own tasks done. They may delay any phone calls or meetings unless they're absolutely necessary in order to be able to complete their own set of responsibilities. This holds true for people that may be trying to lose weight. If they know that junk food is their weakness, instead of having to resist the temptation of eating junk food in their house, they can simply get rid of all the junk food in their house so that they don't have access to it. It is important that you minimize and remove all temptations of the distractions that affect you the most when it comes to reaching your most important goals.

Share Your Goals with Other People

For some people, it may be easier to stick with completing a goal when they have made a public commitment to it. The thought of failing to reach a goal in front of other people can be motivation for the person to stick with it. You can also take this one step further and ask those people to hold you accountable as well. If you aren't sharing your goals with anyone, nobody will know if you have been slacking off from it. When nobody is there to hold you accountable, you will likely be less motivated to keep doing it since nobody will know if you did fail at it.

Use External and Internal Sources of Motivation

There is a saying that goes, "Don't do it for others; do it for yourself." However, some people find that they are much more disciplined when they know that their impulses, emotions, behaviors, and actions affect other people. Contrary to popular belief, it's alright to use external sources to help your motivation. In fact, sometimes, motivation coming from external sources is more powerful than internal motivation. Find the purpose that's beyond yourself that is important to you in order to help give you a higher chance of success.

Discipline Is Created by Creating Habits

We talked about how, when something becomes a habit, you no longer need to draw from your willpower bank to get yourself to do it. For example, if a person's goal was to do more exercise, they should make a commitment to work out for at least 20 minutes per day for a whole month. They will be able to see the benefits of regular exercise if they are able to stick with it. Once they see the benefit, they will have more motivation to keep doing it, and soon it becomes a habit where if this person does not do at least 20 minutes of exercise a day, they don't feel good physically. This way, they will no longer need to draw from their bank of self-control, but instead, exercising for them will naturally come since it has become a habit of theirs.

Why Sacrifice Is A Key To Your Success

Like a physical muscle, there is no shortcut to increased self-discipline. You have to put in the time, effort, and energy if you want to make it happen. With more discipline, you'll see more positive changes in your life. However, you'll need to make sacrifices and adjustments. There will be difficult challenges ahead, but it'll all be worth it.

The road to self-discipline is going to put you to the test and push you beyond your comfort zone. However, it will also make you a much stronger and better person. There is a reason why we often hear successful individuals attribute their success to hard work and self-discipline.

Causes Of Low Self-Discipline

By learning the reasons behind why a person does not take more responsibility for everyday obligations, we are ready to learn some of the causes of poor self-discipline.

Cause #1: Lack of Awareness

The primary cause of low self-discipline is a lack of awareness. This component is important specifically to our imagination and thinking. People are unaware of the thoughts that take our attention are actually negative and can damage a person's well-being. These thoughts are fed into the conscious mind by the negative mind power to ensure that people have minimal time to spend just simply just being mindful. If people are aware of the things that are happening within their own minds, they would know that self-discipline is needed to refocus our attention away from the flow of negative thoughts.

Cause #2: Character Weaknesses

Oftentimes, people who have weak character creates poor self-discipline. This includes aspects that have a low level of inner strength, mental toughness, courage, lack of love for other people, an absence of self-love, low interest in self-improvement, apathy, shortage of responsibility, lack of self-reflection, high levels of greed, and the inability to ignore temptations, in general.

If people place more importance on the desires, thoughts, and emotions that harm them more than the actions, thoughts, and people that help them, it will be difficult for them to develop high self-discipline. Each moment comes with a choice that a person has to make. Either it can be something that helps them reach the goals that they have set for themselves, or they can fall into temptation and choose the action that has instant gratification.

Cause #3: Lack of Ambition

Ambition is very effective in creating self-discipline by giving us a reason to work towards our goals, although we might rather be doing something else. However, it has a negative effect on our self-discipline if our ambition is in an honorable, ethical, or fulfilling one. It is obvious that people who lack the ambition to achieve goals in life will have a harder time building strong self-discipline because they don't have a reason to do it. This is why we deliberated in this segment that one of the main steps in developing strong self-discipline is coming up with clear and attainable goals. By coming up with a goal that is realistic, an individual can then create a plan of action that they can then hold themselves accountable to. They also need to continue finding the motivation and ambition to keep them striving towards their goals.

Cause #4: Having Goals That Have Low Importance

People that have goals that aren't that important tend to lack the ambition to achieve them and, therefore, will not be able to practice their self-discipline. If people set goals that looked good on the outside but didn't actually believe that they were necessary, or didn't see them as goals that are important enough to accomplish in the first place, then they may find it very difficult exercise self-discipline in order to put in the work to achieve them. One of the main motivating factors of self-discipline is having a goal that a person is able to stand by or is important to them. By having an important goal, or something that is meaningful to them, they will be able to find the self-discipline needed in order to complete the tasks required in order to achieve their goal.

Cause #5: Laziness

There are many temporary reasons as to why a person is not exhibiting self-discipline to do the things that need to be done. This could be sickness, tiredness, apathy, or something that is more appealing that is immediately available. If you find that these excuses were often occurring when you were trying to complete the task needed to reach a goal, you need to dig deep and find the real reason why you are choosing options that aren't the ones that will help you achieve your goal. Laziness is often the culprit in a lot of cases. The reasons for laziness usually run very deep into an individual's psyche. If a person believes that there is a goal that is worthwhile, they will be motivated to keep working and applying themselves and making the decisions that make sense when it comes to achieving their goal. However, if they don't have any motivation to achieve their goal, it likely means that their goal isn't important enough, or the person has a natural tendency to be lazy and uninterested.

Cause #6: Lack of Self-Respect

Oftentimes, a person who is lacking self-respect doesn't put a lot of effort or importance in achieving personal excellence. They often don't really care what others think about them or whether they are helping out other people in their lives or not. You might be wondering what self-respect has to do with self-discipline. The answer is that it takes self-discipline in order to produce excellent results, to achieve goals, and to help people who require it. When a person doesn't think about their own self-improvement, they tend to focus on other things that bring them pleasure such as instant gratification. They don't necessarily practice self-discipline because they are comfortable in indulging the instant gratification that life throws at them. If a person lacks respect for themselves, they are more likely to indulge in unhealthy conveniences like fast food or shopping impulses that we conferred. If a person does have self-respect for themselves, they understand that this instant gratification may bring them joy and pleasure at the moment but does very little in helping them achieve healthy long-term goals.

Your Behavior And Its Most Basic Foundations

Many people make the mistake of thinking that forming habits means you are doing the same thing every day. That is simply not true. Think of habits more as character traits, and less as actual actions. For example, you can make it a habit to try to improve yourself each day at work in one specific area. Instead of just assuming you are doing a good job, you can take it upon yourself to look for weaknesses in your performance that can be targeted for improvement. Rather than a specific task or action, the habit in this case is working toward becoming a better employee.

Being habitual is a powerful trait, as long as the habits you form are pushing you to be better than you were yesterday.

Adapt or Die

Staying the same in any walk of life is a recipe for failure. Even if you are good at something, you must adapt your techniques, or you will eventually fall behind. The world is constantly changing, and it is your responsibility to change right along with it. Do you think the SEALs use the same training techniques today as they did when they were formed? Of course not. As science and training techniques have advanced, the SEALs have taken advantage of new innovations to make their teams the best they can be. That doesn't mean the old way of doing it was wrong – it just means that the new way is better.

This is one of the most important lessons that you can take and apply in your own life. Let's say, for example, that you are a terrific salesperson. You connect well with people, you have a great product, and you work hard to close deals day after day. Over the years, you have built a lucrative career on your ability sell to just about anyone. However, as time goes by, you refuse to change. If it worked once, it would work again – at least, that's what you tell yourself.

Of course, as time goes by, your traditional sales methods are less successful. Fewer and fewer people want to buy things in person, as most shopping is now done online. Since you have refused to change, others have taken advantage of the online market and your business soon dries up. Is your failure to blame on the world around you for changing? No – it's on you for not adapting in time.

The Only Easy Day Was Yesterday

On the road to self-discipline, you can't be looking for easy days. Those who are successful in this world – no matter what they happen to be successful in – don't look for easy days. Instead, while others are taking their easy days to rest and recover, the successful are pushing on, finding a way to improve themselves one step at a time. Is it easy? Of course not. Is it rewarding? Absolutely.

Think about it this way – how could you possibly expect to continually get better if today was easier than yesterday? You can't. The only way to improve is if you consistently challenge yourself to complete more and more difficult tasks on an ongoing basis. You need to be waking up in the morning hungry to find the challenge that each day has in store.

Your Hurdles Are Mostly Mental

There is a physical component to anything that you try to accomplish, even if it doesn't have to do with losing weight. For a simple example, even the idea of getting up early in the morning is a physical battle. Your body might be telling you that it wants to keep sleeping, even while your alarm is going off and you know that you should be walking up to get your day started right. However, even while you are waging physical battles against what your body wants to do, it is the battle with your mind that will always determine your fate.

When you think about it, the real purpose behind the rigorous training that the SEALs are put through is to test their mental toughness above all else. It is relatively easy to test physical strength, and it certainly doesn't take 26 weeks to do so. If the Navy SEALs were only interested in finding the most physically fit people available for the job, they wouldn't need to go through the elaborate process that is currently in place to identify those capable of being a SEAL. Instead, they would simply test recruits on things like weightlifting, running, jumping, etc. With the results of a variety of physical tests available, it would be easy to select the most physically fit men among the group. However, those results would do almost nothing to determine who is actually cut out for the incredibly difficult task of being a Navy SEAL.

Instead, the Navy needs to know who is up to the mental challenge of becoming a SEAL. When everything seems stacked against you, and the job seems impossible, how will you respond? How will you deal with adversity when you are faced with a physical task that you don't know if you can complete? Are you going to rise to the occasion or are you going to run away and look for a way out?

These are the questions that the Navy needs to answer when putting potential SEALs through training. They have to be completely sure that each person who earns the designation of a SEAL is going to be up to the challenge of everything that the position requires – both physically and mentally. If a candidate breaks mentally during training, there is no way they will hold up out in the field when the bullets start flying.

Chapter 3. How to Develop Self Discipline

Invest In Self-Regulation

A More Detailed Explanation of Self-Discipline

Self-discipline entails the ability to endure temptations to accomplish set goals, and the essential willpower to carry out a task that needs to be done.

There are thought patterns, emotions, and desires that may hinder your ability to succeed greatly in life. Primarily, self-discipline enables you to disregard everything that would not add positively to the achievement of your goals. Self-discipline is your ability to master your emotions, momentum, cravings, and conduct. In other words, self-discipline enables you to resist the temptation of unnecessary activities. It is the ability to deny momentary pleasures and immediate cravings in the bid to gain long-term satisfaction and fulfillment from achieving better and more profitable goals.

Being a disciplined individual does not entail a restrictive lifestyle or the lack of fun in a person's life. It simply means the art of concentrating your thoughts and strengths on your goals and endure until you see the results.

To be self-disciplined would mean you can make adequate decisions, act, and carry out your major plan regardless of challenges or situations that may seem to hinder you. Self-discipline enables you to attain your goals in a considerable time limit and to live a more orderly and satisfying life.

Self-discipline also means the development of your mind to the degree that it positively influences your choices, rather than by feelings, bad habits, emotions and so on.

Cognition And Its Role In Self-Discipline

The Core Distinctions of Self-discipline

The ability to deny immediate pleasure and cravings in order to achieve a greater good which would require effort and time is the main feature of self-discipline.

Self-discipline is a vital tool for success which can be seen in various ways:
- Endurance
- The ability to carry on and plunge ahead regardless of the shortcomings and failures.
- The willpower to withstand distractions and temptations
- Continuous repetition until you achieve your goals

Difficulties are a major facet of success in life; you can't avoid them. Endurance and doggedness are two other vital ingredients you must have in order to rise above life's difficulties and challenges, and this would definitely require self-discipline.

Self-discipline is beneficial in controlling bad habits such as eating disorders, smoking, drinking and every other kind of negative habit. It is also required for you to be diligent in your study, in developing new skills, in exercise, spiritual development and meditation, and also in mental training.

Effectively utilizing the skill of self-discipline results in self-confidence, healthy self-esteem, and ultimately, it guarantees satisfaction and happiness. However, in the absence of self-discipline, several problems arise in the area of health, failure in achieving the desired goal, relationship problems, and obesity.

Traits Of Self-Disciplined People

Be Calm, Cool and Collected

The first habit that people with mental toughness display that you should try to emulate is that of caring themselves as if they are cool, calm, collected and in control of every situation that they are in. And they do this, even if they are not completely sure that they can control the situation.

Acting and thinking as if you are leaving parts of a situation up to luck and prayer, although this may seem like it brings hope to many people, can cause you to feel that you are not in control of the situation and you are powerless to truly control what is going on around you and the situation that you are in.

Feeling and acting as if you are in control can give you an underlying mindset that you have control over the world around you. This mentality has a significant impact on the way that you think and behave.

Not Wasting Time Concentrating on Things You Cannot Control

In fact, spending a significant amount of time and energy thinking about the things that are beyond your control or that you cannot change can be draining on your energy, frustrating, a waste of time, and a confidence killer. Similar to what they say in Alcoholics Anonymous, "You need to have the courage to accept that the things that you can change and change the things that you can and have the wisdom to know the difference." People with mental toughness tend to abide by this statement even if they have never been an alcoholic. Things that are beyond your control should also be beyond your focus.

No one is blessed with endless mental energy; therefore, one habit that people with mental toughness display is the ability to stop wasting their time thinking about the things that are out of their reach or control so that they can spend more time focusing on all of the things that they have full control over.

This differs from the aforementioned being calm, cool, and collected because you can actually be calm and cool while occupying your mind and your thoughts with activities and events that are not within your control. Stay focused on things that you do have control over.

Leave the Past in the Past but Learn from It

It is easy to understand why you should not spend a great deal of time focused on the past if it was full of negative things. However, many people often fail to realize that it is equally harmful to spend your time focusing on the past it if was great.

Part of understanding that the past is in the past is to understand that you should not bring all of the negative thoughts and feelings and experiences from the past into the present. For instance, if you were the fat girl that did not get many dates in high school and college, however, you lost 75 pounds, you need to understand that you are no longer the fat chick and you should not let the hurts of the past limit your present and future. One way to leave the past in the past is to understand that it does not change. Thus, there is no use in going over different scenarios of what ifs. If there is a different step or direction that you believe you should have gone in in the past, figure out how to go in that direction now. And if the door has closed on that opportunity in your life, find another door that you can open.

Change Yourself but Don't Try to Change Others

In life, we often want other people around us to change so much that we try to change them; however, this is far from a great tactic to us and often a waste of time, energy, and emotions.

If you want to see changes in your life you need to make them. Take active steps to make changes that will benefit you without expecting others to change with you. This is not to say that the people around you that you care about won't be willing to change for the better, but you to see let them make the decision that they need to change on their own.

And even if you can encourage some people to change, you can't change everybody, but you can change some of the people around you. Some people in your life are not going to be willing to change, and if they are bringing you down in any way, you need to get them out of your life. It is important to know when to cut some people out of your life who are treating you negatively or otherwise having a negative effect on your life instead of hoping and waiting for them to change.

Don't Waste Time on Envy and Jealousy

In life, we often look at others and wish we had what they have. Sometimes it seems as though life is unfair because we do not have those things. There is no usefulness in spending time thinking that things are unfair and being jealous of others. In fact, when others around you experience success, you should be happy for them and proud of them in order to be in a positive state of mind. Envy is a significant energy drainer. It is a lot more prudent to spend your time figuring out how you can better yourself than wishing you had what someone else has. If you spend your time thinking about how you can get where you want to be, you may even get what they have that you are jealous of!

Not Spending a Great Deal of Time Worrying About What Others Think About You

Spending time thinking about what others think about you is often in the same category as spending time thinking about things that you cannot control. It can be a major time waster.

Yes, you do need to care what other people think about you. You can't just ignore what other people think about you. In fact, if a significant number of people seem to be thinking the same thing, then they could be right. The world is full of other people, and it is better to have them on your side than against you and can make life significantly easier. You will learn more about this far along in this volume when you learn about emotional intelligence.

Be Thankful for Everything That You Have

People with mental strength garner some of it from being thankful for all that they have. This can especially to true in tough times. Instead of dwelling on the things that you do not have it is often better to focus on the things that you do. This can help you persevere and get through your obstacles and trying times.

Wallowing in self-pity, the opposite of being thankful for what you have is a habit that those who desire or possess mental toughness never display. This is an energy and emotion drainer that can keep you stuck where you are during troubled times, unable to move past them.

This is why you should count your blessings. During hard times or when you need some encouragement, you should even try making a list of the things in your life that you are thankful for. And everything on the list does not have to be something big. Look around at your surroundings and in your life and try to find some small things that you can be thankful for. Noticing all of the little things around you that you can be grateful for that you overlook on a daily basis can help you to understand how lucky and blessed you are and give you the strength and mental toughness to go on day to day and pursue your life's goals.

Don't Criticize

People who are mentally tough don't spend their time complaining about and criticizing situations around them. Instead, they look of the positive aspects of things instead of focusing on the negative.
Either find some way to change whatever it is that you see that's flawed or let it go. Complaining does nothing but causes you and the people around you to hear a bunch of negative thoughts. In fact, if you have a habit of complaining, you may develop the reputation of being a negative force of a downer to people that have to listen to it.

Live in the Present, Not the Future

The present is now. Many people are aware that it is damaging to spend a great deal of time living in the past; however, you may not be as aware that it is just as damaging to spend too much time 'in the future' as well. If there are things that you need to do to achieve your goal, a new goal that you would like to achieve, something that you would like to do, or even something as simple as making sure you do something fun that day, don't wait for a more convenient time in the future to start these things.

Not wanting to live in the future is especially important when it comes to enjoying your life. It is important to take some time out to have fun and enjoy life in order to stay mentally and emotionally balanced. Because everything in life does not always work out as planned and some goals that you set you may not end up achieving, one way to avoid becoming frustrated and lose your willpower and determination is to make sure that you do some of the fun things that you have been waiting until you have more money or until your kids go off to college to do.

Strive to Do What Is Good and Avoid What Is Bad

The daily activities involve making a decision about different issues, and therefore, as you go about your activities remember to be mindful in terms of the choices you make. Remember that every action regardless of whether it is considered important or not, has an ethical or moral component and for you to live a stoic life you must pursue virtue. Therefore, before you make any decision thought the day, make sure that it is directed towards making you virtuous. Put the many options that you have at hand to accomplish the activity and from the options, choose the one that is more moral.

Remember That All You Have Does Not Count

As you go about your daily activities, you must interact with other people from different levels of life, own different opinions, and have different strengths and weaknesses. The people also have different intellectual abilities and from different economic backgrounds. When you meet with them treat them with respect, because all that you have is not yours. Take all your possessions as borrowed things that you can lose any time. The good clothes that you wear, the food that you eat, the good health that you are enjoying, and all other possession including the people that you love should not be a basis for you to demean others; they can vanish in a fraction of a second. Therefore, regardless of your achievements, possession, and titles or the position you hold in whatever place, you are just a small thing on earth, which can vanish from the earth the effect felt by the whole world is small. Remember that even the prominent people die, and it is only their names that are left in accounts to be read by people in the future generations. Therefore, as you mingle with people of different levels in different aspects remain focused; do not think of yourself highly because all of you are the same.

Take Time to Experience Hardship

There are conditions that you fear experiencing in your life, and because you know them, let yourself experience them bit by bit in your daily activities. For example, if you fear being demoted from the position you have to work as an ordinary worker, you can choose the activities done by the ordinary worker, and have a schedule that will help you do the tasks they do every day. The approach will help you appreciate the work done by the junior workers and deal with the anxiety and fear of losing the position that you have. The experience makes you realize that being at a lower position is not that bad, and because you have already lived it, it will be easy to cope in case it happens to you. The consistent discomfort that you feel when you practice being in hardship each day also brings about mental and physical endurance, and if a worst-case scenario comes your way, it will not leave you wretched.

Looking at Situation in the Wider Perspective

It is not always that we are happy or the events and situations that come our way in our daily activities are appealing; disappointment happens every day, and they can shut us from seeing the bright future that we have. When you are a disappointment, it does not matter the activity that has led to your disappointment with the person who has disappointed you. Sit down and look at yourself and what you are worth, and the life that you would wish to live in the future, and ask yourself, is looking miserable because of one person or one event in your life a good option. Count the blessing that surrounds you, and they cannot be compared to one disappointment. Therefore, always look at the future and not the past; the future can be made better, past time and all its activities cannot be rewound and made better. There is no need to dwell on the past, but the coming activities have greater potential. As a stoic always, take each opportunity in your routine seriously to improve your future.

Anticipating Negative Happenings

Before you begin your day, you have all the activities set. However, you should reflect on the plan for each activity and all the requirements for its effectiveness. As you evaluate, also look at the possibility of the activities failing or not going as you have planned. Also, anticipate the causes of the failure and look for measures to prevent it from falling. This might sound as being pessimistic, but it will save you from experiencing the actual failure because you have everything in place to prevent failure. In addition, since you are prepared for the failure, if it happens it does not affect you much. Therefore, in every plan that you have for the day, always anticipate negative happenings, and prepare for them by having measures to prevent them from happening.

Chapter 4. Daily Self-Discipline

Improving Concentration

For most of us, managing our time becomes such a challenge day by day that it will ultimately affect our productivity. We can't seem to reduce the number of tasks that keep piling on our to-do-list, and we just keep getting bombarded with emails, write-ups, reports, and not to mention our own personal and household responsibilities.

In 1955, in an essay by Cyril Northcote Parkinson, he coined a phrase known as the "Parkinson Law." He states that "work expands so as to fill the time available for its completion." What this means is that the more time we allocate for completing a task or project, we end up taking more time to complete it. Hence, many at times, we feel that we can't complete a task even if we thought we had given ourselves ample time to work on it. In the end, the only way we can negate this is to put stricter deadlines and really push yourself to complete them. That's where the "Pomodoro Technique" comes in to play.

This technique is a time management technique that focuses on grouping tasks into a 25-minute window of time. For each 25-minute time window, you will be allocated a 5-minute break. Once you complete four 25-minute windows in succession, you are allowed a longer break, which is usually between 15 to 30 minutes. This system was introduced in the late 1980's by a man called Francesco Cirillo.

This system works because instead of focusing on one particular task for an extended period of time, you actually break it down to smaller, manageable windows. Also, with the smaller time frame, you will be less tempted to break away and do other unwanted tasks such as checking your email, going through social media, or any other distracting activity. Through the Pomodoro Technique, you will find that you end up getting your tasks completed due to this newfound sense of urgency, you will be able to focus on the task at hand, you avoid multitasking completely, reduce your stress levels, and you will also increase your determination and concentration in completing a task.

Building Mental Toughness

Mental strength is one of the most important elements of self-discipline. Knowing how it contributes to self-discipline will help you to see why you need to be constantly working to enhance it.

When you are mentally strong, it allows you to conquer self-doubt so that it is not able to interfere with your level of discipline or cause you to procrastinate out of fear.

Motivation comes from your mental strength. When you are not mentally strong, you will find that it is much easier to lose your motivation before you even have a chance to take full advantage of it.

You can easily tune out comments and advice that are simply not going to help you. This is critical for self-discipline since it is all about efficiency and removing unnecessary baggage.

When you are mentally strong, you are able to face your fears. Fears are one of the biggest reasons that people are not able to develop a strong sense of self-discipline.

You can more easily rebound from failure with mental strength. When you quickly come back from failure, it's more difficult to disrupt your ability to be disciplined.

Finally, you can easily learn from your mistakes. Remember that learning and accountability are paramount when working to enhance your discipline level.

Control Your Mind

Accepting What Happens

In a daily routine, sometimes things do not happen the way we have planned, this is because even though we plan for the daily activities, we do not have control of the way they would happen. Therefore, as you plan to keep in mind it might not be as planned, and if it happens as planned be happy about it, and if it does not happen as planned again be happy about it. There are things which are meant to happen the way they do, and even if you plan and take all the measures to make sure they happen as you wish; they still do not happen as expected. This means fate controls such situations, and it is good to accept them the way they happen. The attitude will help you not to spend much energy on things that cannot change, and not be frustrated when things do not happen as you wish. There is a reason that they happen the way they do, and even if you do not know the reason, it is always for the best.

Turning Problems into Blessings

It is not always that we encounter good experiences, there are bad experiences that come our way, and sometimes we ask ourselves why it should be me. When the experience is not good you should always learn to step on it and find a good experience from it. For instance, when going to work, you can meet people who step on you and just go away without apologizing. When you reach the workplace, the boss yells at you for no good reason. It seems unfair, but you can look at it as an opportunity to be more tolerant. Therefore, when you face a challenge in your daily routine, do not feel like, why me; take it as an opportunity to make yourself a better person.

Finally, if you are a perfectionist, you are holding yourself back big time. Being a perfectionist is actually common, particularly because as kids, we are taught to do our best and to strive to be the best, and in many cases, we are not given adequate attention unless we are excelling beyond our peers. Learning to give up your perfectionist streak and start focusing on just getting things done is a great way to step past this habit and into one that is actually going to help you. Naturally, you do not want to have your progress completely squashed by lowering your expectations of yourself or your self-standards down to practically nothing, but you also don't want them too high. A great strategy is to aim to have everything accomplished at what you would consider being 80% of the way to your idea of perfection. This way, you are putting in significant effort and you are creating success, and you are holding yourself back by trying to be the best of the best.

Building On Your Good Habits And Getting Rid Of Negative Ones

If you find that your productivity is really being destroyed by your own bad habits, it may be time for you to begin developing positive habits that are going to replace these bad habits. Learning how to replace your productivity-busting habits with new habits that are going to help you boost your productivity and increase your self-discipline overall can help you begin to develop a deeper sense of self-discipline. This way, you are also able to become more productive and achieve more overall. In the end, your habits can begin to serve you rather than prevent you from achieving your desires, which leads to a greater capacity to create all that you desire.

As you well know by now, we have already touched deep on habits and how habits can be either negative or positive. At this point, you are well aware of how habits work and what they can be used for if you are using them properly. So, at this point, if you are still fostering bad habits that are killing your productivity, there is a strong chance that this is because you do not yet know what these bad habits are or how or why they are killing your productivity. Learning how to bring these habits into your awareness and discern which ones are bad and which ones are not is a great opportunity for you to begin developing awareness around how you can start swapping out your bad habits for ones that actually produce positive and wanted results.

The first and most common bad habit that people tend to engage in is being ineffective in creating priorities in their schedules. The truth is: not everything is as important as everything else on your schedule. There are some things that are going to require your time more than others, and you are going to have to learn how to balance your schedule to ensure that these more important things are being addressed in a timely manner. For example, going to your third dinner with friends this week is probably less important than getting to the doctor to find out why you are not feeling well lately. Although one may be more fun than the other, and you may justify it by saying it is a networking event or by saying that you need to be spending time with friends, you are also procrastinating by not having priorities. Set your priorities effectively and watch as the rest of your schedule falls into place.

If you are keeping the bigger picture in mind to the point where you are no longer being productive, you are holding onto a bad habit. A lot of people have a bad habit of looking at the big picture in the midst of actually attempting to work which leads to them having a hard time getting focused on each actual task that needs to get done. This can create feelings of overwhelm and intimidation, as well as apathy and passiveness, depending on how you are looking at the bigger picture. In other words, if you are looking at the big picture in any way that is preventing you from progressing in life, you are looking at it ineffectively and at the wrong times. Limit your big picture thinking to times when you are not working so that you can stay focused on your work and get plenty done when you are actually working.

Another bad habit that people tend to have that they do not even realize is not having a work routine. If you are into working whenever you feel like working, you are setting yourself up for disaster because you are probably never going to feel like working. It is hard to get your mind ready and engaged if you are not actually holding onto a routine since your mind is unaware of what the triggers are that determine it is time to get into a work mentality. Learning how to swap out your go-with-the-flow attitude for one that helps you actually hold onto a specific routine is a great opportunity for you to begin getting more done.

Build Up Your Daily Routine

Self-discipline is nothing more than practicing a series of good habits until they become ingrained in the daily routine to the point where they are a part of life. As more bad habits are replaced with good habits, then the good ones take over and lead to a more orderly and organized life. As life becomes more organized, it becomes easier to manage—and now, it has become a life of self-discipline.

Forming Good Habits And Breaking Bad Habits

Developing good habits really is as simple as knowing where the shoes are. A self-disciplined person would have a dedicated space for shoes. When the shoes are removed from the feet they are placed in this dedicated space. The self-disciplined person is never almost late to work because they cannot find their shoes. If this sounds familiar, then try this little exercise. Pick a dedicated place for the shoes. It does not matter where; the closet, tucked under the bed, next to the nightstand, wherever. The dedicated spot is a personal choice. Now, every night, make a conscious effort to put the shoes in the dedicated spot every time they are removed from the feet. One day, it will be apparent that this has become a habit—a good habit to have—because now, there is no more searching for the shoes on cold, dark mornings. While this exercise may seem quite simple, it is a prime example of setting a goal, making a plan to achieve that goal, and achieving that goal.

The problem is the pathways in our brains. Whenever a habit is begun, whether it is a good habit or a bad habit, the brain creates pathways that tell the body to act a certain way when certain things happen. A cigarette smoker will want to light up a cigarette when someone else does. Seeing the cigarette, smelling the cigarette, triggers the nerve pathways in the brain of a smoker to have their own cigarette. This is why cigarette smokers who are trying to quit are often encouraged to change some of their daily habits. Smoking is often tied to other activities. Beer drinkers who smoke will smoke more when drinking. Coffee drinkers who smoke will automatically light up while pouring that first morning cup. People who smoke on long car trips may be encouraged to chew gum instead. People who drink may need to stop frequenting the local bar. Coffee drinkers will need to find something to do with their hands instead of lighting a cigarette. The nerve pathways that the bad habit created can be broken. It will take time and hard work. But then NOT smoking becomes the new good habit.

Creating good habits from bad requires effort but it can be done. Good habits take time to build and bad habits take time to break. Start small, work hard and consider a few simple tricks that might help ease into the habit of fostering good habits.

Start by taking the time to be thankful for what is already present in life. Humans spend much more time than needed wanting bigger, better things. Once people learn to be happy with the things they already have and not waste time wanting things they do not have, they can begin to see what is really important in life and begin to make a plan to add to those things that are really meaningful.

Humans spend far too much time feeling useless emotions like guilt or anger. Negative emotions use way too much energy that is needed to focus on the good things in life. Letting go of negative emotions frees the mind, the heart, and the soul to be able to focus on the positive effects that building new habits will create. Learning how to let go of negative emotions is actually an excellent way to build self-discipline. It is a way of letting the world see the strength inside.

Remember to eat healthily and sleep well and regularly. The body cannot process new habits if it is undernourished. Good healthy food is crucial to giving the body enough energy to work on new and better habits. This is especially necessary when trying to break bad habits. Bad habits require extra energy to put aside. Sleep is especially important too. Most adults need between seven and nine hours of sleep every night. Play around with these numbers until the correct amount is determined, and then stick to that number. Make every attempt to go to bed at the same time each night and wake up at the same time each day. This is a good habit that will lead to self-discipline of personal habits. Of course, things happen, and sometime people fall off the schedule. But get back on it as soon as possible and do not regret one or two small slips. They happen.

Practice organization. Some people are naturally organized, and some people need to work very hard to be organized. If the latter group seems more familiar, do not try to become completely organized overnight. The organization will not happen, but failure definitely will. Being well organized is a habit—and like any other good habit, it will take work to achieve. Begin by organizing one thing. Begin with a drawer. It is small and easy to organize. Have some boxes ready. When removing things from the drawer look at them closely and try to recall the past time they were used. If it has been more than six months, then the item is not needed. Have some boxes ready while doing this. If the item is still in good condition it goes in the box to be donated. If the item is beyond usefulness, then it goes into the box to go to the trash. Be firm! Do not hold onto something because it might get used.

Track Your Progress

Self-discipline is a work-in-progress and a goal. The goal is to become more self-disciplined. However, being self-disciplined is not something one achieves once and considers it done. Once self-discipline is achieved, it must be considered a lifestyle—it must be nurtured daily and constantly refreshed to stay relevant and useful. Self-discipline is a habit—a good habit to have to make life more worthwhile.

Self-discipline is the backbone of a successful person. Whether a person desires personal success, professional success, or both, self-discipline will lead them to their goal. It begins with a strong ability to control oneself with strict discipline. Thoughts are under control. Emotions are under control. Behavior is under control. This does not mean that thoughts never run wild and emotions never flow to the surface. It just means that they are never allowed to control the person. One might get a little misty eyed at the birthday card with the cute kittens on it, but one would not let this feeling take over the entire day. This is self-discipline. The person controls thoughts and emotions. Self-control becomes a habit—a new personal best friend.

Chapter 5. Important Techniques

Techniques That Ensure Optimal Productivity

A big reason for why you want to develop your self-discipline is likely because you want to increase your own productivity. Being able to get more done means that you are more likely to achieve higher levels of success in virtually every area of your life which, if managed properly, can lead to greater happiness, reduced stress, and more joy overall. You can achieve that by developing techniques that actually improve your productivity and practicing self-discipline to ensure that you are always staying on track with these techniques.

One of the best ways to increase your productivity and develop your self-discipline is actually to become very diligent about taking breaks and ensuring that you regularly have downtime. Many people think that the key to doing more is doing more, but this actually leads to lower energy levels and reduced mental clarity due to exhaustion, frustration, and unmet needs. If you are finding that your own productivity levels are low, taking a break and using this break to increase your energy levels is a great opportunity for you to increase your productivity in the end. Regularly scheduling breaks and ensuring that you fully break during that time is a great opportunity for you to get what you need by allowing yourself to engage in a healthy practice of stress management.

Another great way to increase productivity and develop your self-discipline is to learn how to eliminate any and all distractions that are notorious for breaking your productivity levels. For example, if you keep your phone on and around at all times, you may find that instead of getting important tasks done, you are checking social media or texting your friends. Naturally, this will decrease your productivity levels and reduce your capacity to achieve your goals. If, however, you were to set those distractions aside you could begin focusing completely on the task at hand and getting a lot more done in significantly shorter windows of time.

If you are looking to boost your productivity naturally, you can also engage in various practices that are known for naturally boosting your energy. Things like listening to music that boost your energy levels, having a healthy diet, and consistently working out allow you to increase your energy levels naturally so that you have more energy to contribute to important tasks. This way, you are not dragging your feet or slacking off when you are working due to being tired or lacking energy, but instead, you are creating an increase of energy that you can use to get ahead with.

To continually improve your productivity, another great method is to focus on developing your self-awareness around productivity specifically. By paying attention to how you are already productive and where you may be lacking in productivity, you can help yourself begin to find new ways that you can improve your personal productivity. Improving your productivity this way will not only bring you forward on your own growth toward becoming more productive, but it will also support you in your self-discipline by teaching you how to critically assess your own behaviors. This way, you can begin finding new and improved ways to heal your own behavioral patterns so that you are taking actions that actually serve your growth. Remember, learning to become more self-aware and self-disciplined in any area of your life, such as with productivity, will help you improve in other areas of your life, too.

Finally, another great way to improve your productivity is to actually outsource some of your work to other people who can do it. Sometimes, we attempt to take on far too much work ourselves which can lead to having too much on our own plates, making it hard for us to be productive because there is simply too much to do. This way, even if you think you are getting everything done and you are being productive, it can feel like you are not because your to-do list does not feel like it is getting any smaller. If you were to outsource your tasks, however, such as by hiring an assistant or having family members take some of the tasks off of your list, you could begin having more free time to get everything done. This way, you are no longer feeling trapped with so much to do but instead, you are able to get everything done reasonably, and with the help of other people who can just as easily be doing the tasks that you were taking onto your own shoulders.

Techniques For Developing Greater Self-Discipline

Immerse Yourself in the Culture of Self-Discipline

Surround Yourself with Disciplined People

When developing your own self-discipline, you need to surround yourself with people who have the same goals and aspirations as you. It is even better if you can find people who are very dedicated to their work. By surrounding yourself with these types of people, you will have someone with which you can compare yourself. If you are competitive by nature, having people around you who are good at what they do can ignite your competitive spirit. This can be a great source of extrinsic motivation.

Examine Your Internal Beliefs

Your internal beliefs, ideas, and attitude set the tone for your success and life in general. The saddest part about these beliefs is that they are so deeply ingrained in our subconscious mind that we are often unaware of them. These ideas may be sown in our mind since a very young change through childhood experiences or tough situations within our family or immediate environment. For instance, if your caregivers pressurized you with high expectations and made you feel small if you were unable to meet them, you may have grown up with the belief that you are good for nothing.

Build an Attitude of Gratitude

One of the strategies to attract even more in your life is to be thankful for what you already have. This is one of the best ways to condition your subconscious for success. Counting your blessings allows you to curb more negative, self-defeating, and hopeless thoughts and beliefs, and discipline your thinking for success. It is time to turn your negative thinking upside down and be grateful for all the gifts you have been blessed with. It will change the frequency of your thoughts from negative and self-limiting to more positive, constructive and hopeful.

Build a Mindset of Converting Challenges into Opportunities

Contrary to popularly held beliefs, winners are not folks who have never experienced setbacks or failures. In fact, they are individuals who turn these challenges upside down into learning opportunities.

Decide to Transform

If you are unhappy with your life, money, or professional life, start by changing your habits, actions, mindset, thoughts, behavior, attitude, and so on now.

All you require to be rich and successful is within you. It is inside you, waiting to be tapped. You just have to dip into it to experience roaring huge success. At times, we wonder why talented and passionate people are unable to achieve improvement and success, while other people who may not be as skilled witness greater success and glory. It is merely a matter of mindset that drives people to work hard and chase their dreams despite challenges. Perseverance is often the clinching factor between success and failure.

Chapter 6. Utilization and Application of Positive Habits

The Importance Of Identifying Bad Habits

When you have bad habits, you will tend to always default to those bad habits. You may fail to follow through with what you have said you would do because you are always making excuses, and that is just second nature for you. No matter the reason behind your bad habits, you will find that you fail to do what is expected or what you want to do on a regular basis because your default state is to procrastinate or avoid whatever it is that you should be doing in the first place.

This is exactly why you need more than a good mindset in order to successfully self-discipline. You need to figure out the habits that can make your self-discipline a regular occurrence in your life, as without those habits, you are going to struggle to come up with the necessary behaviors that will support it. You can talk the talk all you want, telling yourself that you will be self-disciplined and setting up the mindset for that self-discipline, but until you are actively following through with whatever you have said that you will be doing, you are not truly self-disciplined. That self-discipline comes with time and real, legitimate effort. You are not actually self-disciplined until you are acting accordingly.

Exploring Habits And Their Impact On Self-Control

What to Tell Yourself When You Feel like Giving in to Temptations or Indulgences

It Is up to Me

In climbing the ladder of success, there is only you. The people you love most and who love you and want to see you succeed are motivators. Ultimately, the choice is yours whether to stay put or to move on. The choice is yours on which advice to listen to or which opportunity to look into. Only you can choose how you spend your time, who you spend your time with and what decisions you want to make. You cannot blame someone else for your misgivings and your shortcomings. Even if you do not have direct control over something, the choice is ultimately yours to respond. So, remember, 'it is up to me' on how you choose this day to be.

This is Necessary

The biggest enemy to success is the path to less resistance. We keep hearing this over and over and over again about how people who are successful did not get there easily. They had to rinse, repeat plenty of times before they finally hit their big break. This is why every time you hit a roadblock, remember that every great victory requires great sacrifice. If you choose the fun and easy over the necessary, you will never reach the levels of success and happiness you are capable of achieving in life. If success was easy, everybody would attain it. You need to remind yourself each time you are faced with the possibility of breaking your routine or your habit, 'I must do what is necessary.'

I Will Never Give Up

We talked about how to make a commitment to change and also writing down our personal mission and even creating a mood board. We also talked about daily targets to hit. When you do all these things, keep reminding yourself that no matter what, 'I will never give up.' Repeat this day in, day out.

Does This Mean That Self-Disciplined People Are Always 100% Disciplined?

Self-disciplined people know what they want in life, and because they know what their goals and targets are and how to get them, they live a more fulfilled life. And this can be you. By knowing your Why, creating a personal commitment to change and sticking to it, you will lead a more fulfilling life.

But what if you have one of those days where you just do not want to do routine? If everything in your day just went wrong and all you want to do is take a hot shower, get into comfy pajamas, and curl up in bed, foregoing your 10 minutes of workout or even that 5 minutes of meditation, or writing in your journal to reflect?

We all have those days. Which is also why it is important to include self-care and self-love routines and even schedule sloppy time into our self-discipline habits.

Scheduling Slop Time
Taking a break is an essential part of making sure your self-discipline stays sustainable. In anything that we do, taking a break or rest brings more rewards than downsides. We shall call this our slop time.

Slop time is when you do not need to focus on our goal or what you need to do tomorrow. It is the time when you can allow yourself to cheat on it or not do it at all. We are humans, and we are bound to do it anyway, so you might as well allow yourself that space to do something outside your routine or daily habits.

During your slop time:

- Don't look at your journal
- Don't think about what you need to do the next day or what your goals and targets are.
- Schedule your slop time during weekends or even mid-week. Whatever works for you as long as you do not do the same things that you do on an everyday basis.

Bend the rules a little bit. Instead of always making your bed, maybe you can skip this and instead go straight to making your coffee and sitting down to watch some TV. If eating a salad for lunch is something you do every day, you can bend the rules and eat a cheeseburger instead. Your slop time can be a few hours or a full day. This is up to you so long as you give yourself a start time and end time. If your slop time is scheduled every weekend because weekends are for the family, then give yourself time, from 7am Saturday morning to 7pm Sunday evening, I will do things I do not normally do on my daily routine.

Allowing slop time is crucial because it prevents us from feeling dejected or get bored or hitting a plateau in our self-discipline journey.

Temporarily ignoring a goal for a short period of time (like during the weekend) is great to refocus your energy and do things better when you start the next week fresh. Just remember not to over-do it and don't make this a habit. Slop times are good if it is done once or twice a month.

Creating Your Self-Care Ritual
Most of what you would consider in this self-care ritual are the things that you consider You time. It is simply just time you put aside to focus on yourself, and scheduling this You time is a key habit in self-discipline. Having these rituals on and off is a great way for you to

focus on your own wellbeing and just give your mind a respite in the midst of all your routine and goal setting. How you do it, for how long, what it is, and how easy it is for you entirely depends on you, your lifestyle, your situation, and your preference. We have a few ideas for you, but first, let us look at how you can create your very own self-love ritual.

This self-care ritual should only be confined to days when you are emotionally, mentally, and physically worn out, tired, and just need to destress to reset your mind. It is a temporary relief to get the negativity out of our system so we can refocus again and look at things more objectively.

If I had 5 minutes to myself, I would like to:	If I had 10 minutes to myself, I would like to:	If I had 30 minutes to myself, I would like to:
- Put on a face mask	- Meditate - Sing out loud in the shower	- Do a HIIT workout

- Have a cup of hot tea - Sit quietly in my car - Listen to some music - Massage my feet - Eat an Ice cream	- Do a few stretches - Sleep - Call a friend to talk - Have a glass of wine	- Practice some yoga - Have a bowl of ramen - Have a nice hot bath - Bake a cake - Go for a run

Habits To Become More Productive

Becoming more productive begins by learning how to delay your gratification and work together with yourself to overcome procrastination tendencies. Eliminating the blocks that are preventing you from achieving productivity is a great first step to overcome anything that is holding you back from success. Then, learning how to develop habits that are actually going to move you forward will really help you take off and achieve an entirely new level of success in your life. This is going to take you from gradually stumbling forward to launching forward full throttle toward your increased productivity and, therefore, more consistent achievements in your life.

Like with procrastination and gratification, productivity is actually a habit. You either have the habit of being productive, or you do not. If you have been procrastinating and engaging in instant gratification up until now, chances are you are not working on developing habits around productivity yet because you have been working against them, instead. The best thing is, now that you have eliminated the blocks on your productivity, developing these habits is actually going to be significantly easier. At this point, you have already begun to discover how habits work and you have seen firsthand how you can shift your habitual behaviors to begin achieving better results. Now, you are going to continue on that path to develop your productivity and, in turn, have better results from your efforts.

Becoming More Persistent

Persistence is another vital habit that you need to develop if you want to be a disciplined person.

Persistence is continuing with your tasks despite the adversities. It is not giving up despite naysayers, unfortunate events, and other negative factors.

You have to keep in mind that failure is inevitable. Everybody fails at some point in their lives. Even the most successful people have failed. In fact, they have probably failed more times than you have. You just do not know about their sacrifices and failures because their success overshadows these aspects.

When you try something or take risks, there is a high possibility that you may fail. For example, starting a business can set you up for bankruptcy. However, it can also set you up for success and prosperity. If you are persistent, the possibility of failure does not matter. It does not deter you from pursuing your objectives.

With persistence, you can always get back on your feet and continue your journey. You are aware that there might be more failures along the way, but you are fine with it. Persistence allows you to form self-discipline. When you really want to achieve something, you condition your mind and body. In other words, you discipline yourself so that you can attain this goal. Achieving your goals can be hard, and on the other hand, it is easy to get unmotivated. It is much more convenient to give up than to push through. This is especially true if you are already experiencing so much pain and pressure. Then again, you should think of your end goal. The pain and sufferings that you experience now will all be worth it once you achieve your goal. Persistence is an energy that a self-disciplined person possesses great power. Increasing your capacity to engage in self-discipline through developing a greater persistence is a powerful way to keep yourself moving forward even when obstacles are thrown in your path. See, the key here is to understand that obstacles will always exist and that you are always going to be exposed to dealing with obstacles in your life. Just because you make up your mind about something does not mean that you are not going to have any challenges to face around that thing. Instead, it means that you are going to have challenges to face but, hopefully, you are also going to have more reason to persist and push through those challenges so that they no longer hold you back.

The first step in developing your persistence is having a vision that is far bigger than just yourself. When we have something that we are clearly working toward, it becomes easier for us to persist because we are no longer attempting to achieve something only on behalf of ourselves. Instead, we are attempting to achieve something because we can see how it is going to benefit ourselves and others, which leads us to feel like there is a bigger reason behind what we are trying to achieve. This way, we do not find it so easy to talk ourselves out of moving forward because there is a lot more at stake. Now, rather than saying "I won't be that disappointed if this never happens," we can say "I don't want them to be so disappointed if I don't." We have given ourselves a strong purpose and, as such, we have also encouraged ourselves to work harder and move forward with greater triumph to achieve our goals. Now, you really have a reason to keep going, and as long as you have picked a reason that we value, there is no way that you are slowing down.

Another great way to develop your persistence is to develop a support team. Although you do not want to rely exclusively on your support team to grow and gain what you are seeking, learning how to have a support team in place for when you need an added boost is powerful. What I mean is, do not build a support team expecting that they are going to do all of the work for you and all you have to do is sit back and direct everyone on what needs to be done. This is called procrastination and passing the blame, and it is certainly not a sign of self-discipline. However, having a support team who can motivate you, inspire you, and help you through challenges when you are truly stuck is powerful. This way, you know that you are not alone and therefore your challenges and goals do not seem quite so intimidating: because you can easily lean back on the support available to you as needed.

Persistence can also be developed through the use of a schedule which can help motivate you to keep going. For many people, persistence begins to break down when they hit a challenge because they then begin to procrastinate and put things off. Having your task scheduled on a calendar, however, motivates you to keep going because it allows you to stay focused on how you can continue to develop and advance, at least for a period of time. This way, even if you are progressing slowly, you are still progressing rather than putting it off and saying that you will do it far ahead, even though far ahead never comes.

Another great way to develop persistence is to teach others, which allows you to feel as though the information you have gained and the knowledge that you have is truly valuable. When you teach others, you anchor the knowledge within yourself and you also inspire yourself to dig deeper and learn more. This way, your knowledge feels useful and you are actually stimulated to begin learning about how you can apply that knowledge in other ways. For many people, this can help move you through blocks and inspire you to find new answers so that you can continue developing and growing down your own path.

Finally, in addition to making it bigger than yourself, you can also make the stakes higher. The higher the stakes are on something that you want to accomplish, the more likely you are going to want to accomplish it. For example, if someone told you that you could earn $15 doing something, you would likely find it easy to make it meaningless if you really did not want to do it. Alternatively, if someone told you that you could earn $1,500 doing something, now they have captured your attention and you are more interested in earning money through the task. Upping the stakes is a great opportunity for you to shift into wanting to find a way through virtually anything that you are going through because it inspires you to feel like you have more to gain – or to lose – with that task.

A burning desire to achieve these goals will not be enough to achieve these goals. Strong knowledge of personal strengths and weaknesses combined with a good understanding of how to discipline oneself is the key to being successful. Good habits make the difference between failure and success.

Successful people know that discipline is the key that unlocks the door to future goal achievement. They use discipline daily to enable themselves to be able to achieve their dreams. They know how to use a strong foundation built on strong habits to enable them to be successful. They are fully aware that self-discipline will allow them to accomplish more in less time—making them a more valuable member of the team.

But where does this discipline come from? How does one person seem so at-ease with controlling their actions and behaviors while other people fail on a daily basis? How do some people live lives of total self-control, while other people never seem to know where their shoes are, much less where they are going? The answer is habit. Behavior is mostly driven by habit. If someone can control their habits, they can have strict control over their personal habits.

Chapter 7. Mental Toughness and Personal Goals

How To Build Mental Toughness

Develop a strong support system

Create a positive, strong, and encouraging support system to gain strength from whenever required. During challenging times, we must be able to share our feelings with a close, trustworthy, and motivating group of people. Exchange thoughts and feelings, enlist the support of people you trust, learn about people's journey, gain constructive feedback, enlist support, and discuss possible alternatives. The people you surround yourself with contribute largely to your thoughts and mental framework. Speaking to trusted people can help you gain new insights, views, and solutions about challenging situations, which in turn boosts your mental toughness.

Take cold showers

You might think this is unnecessary suffering, but it is not because taking cold showers has a lot of benefits such as boosting your immune system, increasing levels of testosterone, reducing inflammation, and so on. When the cold water touches your skin for the first time, try not to yell or wince. Just bear it and keep your mind and body as relaxed as possible by taking deep breaths. Try to stay in the cold water for at least 30 seconds and just make it longer as you get used to the coldness.

Minimize social media usage

It takes a lot of mental toughness to unplug from social media. You can either stop using it completely or try to use it only when necessary, like for communication or sharing important stuff. But minimize social media usage as much as you can and just spend your free time doing more productive things. Believe it or not, Steve Jobs didn't let his kids use iPads because he knows how toxic it can get once people start to go online and use social media.

Get out of bed right away

When you hear your alarm go off in the morning, do not press the snooze button, and do not stay in your bed even for just one minute longer. Get out of bed right away and do something to keep your blood flowing. Splash your face with cold water, make coffee or tea, prepare breakfast, and just do anything to wake yourself up. This is all just mind over matter. And you will feel a lot better in the future on when you realize how much you were able to finish in a day because you woke up early.

Sleep on the floor

You can also try sleeping on the floor once in a while. You don't necessarily need to give up your comfortable bed for good. Just do this from time to time to help you build your mental toughness. For a really tough challenge, sleep without a blanket. Use a thin sheet if you are not ready for the difficulty level.

Do small exercises

This will not be your regular full-blown workout. That is another thing that you should be doing even if you are not trying to lose weight because it will keep your body strong and healthy. These mini workouts are workouts that you can incorporate in your everyday life.

Move slowly

You might think that this tip is counterintuitive, because slowness is often not associated with success and achieving goals. But this does not literally mean working at a slower pace. It just means that you do not make impulsive actions and snap decisions.

Get dirty

Some people are so afraid to get themselves dirty because getting dirty is way out of their comfort zone. Although being clean is something that we should all strive for, there is nothing wrong with getting yourself dirty from time to time.

Read

Reading a manuscript can make you tougher mentally because it helps you improve your mental focus for a long period of time. Read a volume for a couple of hours every day; that can teach you a thing or two about delayed gratification, unlike television and online videos that are passive entertainment and do not really contribute anything to improving your mental toughness. Reading is also an activity that allows you to use your mind active and learning new words and information is always a welcome bonus.

Take a break

When something doesn't help you achieve the desired results, go on a break or change your strategy rather than giving up. Tackle the task with a rejuvenated, fresher, and brand-new perspective after recharging your batteries. True success and glory come to people who do not quit.

Build a mindset

When faced with tough situations, brainstorm. Think of solutions, ideas, alternatives, and possibilities for resolving the situation instead of giving up. There are various ways to work out a solution strategy by keeping your mind more open, flexible, and fearless. You may require a change in the approach or a slight strategy change. Recognize various ways to deal with a challenging or overwhelming situation.

Your Personal Goals

Successful and high-performing individuals are not exempted from the many challenges and obstacles in life. Just like everyone else, they experience failures, exhaustion, burnout, rejection, and pain. What set them apart are their abilities to soldier on, and to remain focused on their personal goals.

How is this possible?

Many studies point out that mental strength is one of most significant factors that determine the level of success that a person can attain in life. Also referred to as mental toughness, it is not something that you are born with though. Some studies indicate the role of genetics on one's predisposition towards becoming a mentally strong person, but much of what is known about this concept strongly proves this: Everyone is capable of developing a high level of mental strength.

Given this, the segment below discusses the various ways on how you can attain success through the development of your mental strength. Keep in mind, however, that there is no universal formula or step-by-step guide that could totally work for you.

Each of the methods described below come with high recommendations from experts, but the best way to go about this is get to know your options, conduct an examination of your current capabilities vis-à-vis your goals, and then create a strategy and an action plan that you believe would work well for you.

Your Overall Happiness

Achieving Happiness

Persistence may be the key to self-discipline, but happiness is the result. You unlock the door to your happiness when you give yourself what you truly want. And how do you get what you truly want? By using self-discipline to reach your goals of success to make all of your life dreams come true. All of the energy you put into making your life the one that you want isn't hard when it's what you are truly wanting and desiring for yourself. Your whole life's happiness comes from being yourself and living the life of your dreams.

Being in a culture that demands so much of us, we can lose sight of what matters most. You might look at all of the people in your life and think that they have it better than you and you long for that perfect house and have the job of your dreams with the partner you have always wanted to meet and start a life with. Also, you could be looking for the complete opposite of that because you already had that life and it turned out that it wasn't what you wanted after all. We all have a life dream, and we all need to arrive there somehow. And it doesn't have to look anything like someone else's fantasy at all in order to be successful for you.

Bringing a little self-discipline into your life can have a major impact on your happiness and quality of life. It can be a simple matter that isn't about achieving an ultimate life dream. Your happiness could come from staying on track with your diet and losing ten pounds; it could be that you started waking up an hour earlier than before so you could practice yoga and you are feeling better in your body as a result. The little wins are just as meaningful and important as the big ones, and all of them lead to happiness with yourself and your life overall.

It has been proven that self-discipline creates the sensation of happiness because it is its own reward. Now consider the fact that self-discipline is a reward for doing what you said you would, and that leads to a sense of confidence, self-worth, achievement, and higher self-esteem.

Let's consider the research on the matter. Often we consider of the self-disciplined as being Puritanical or completely unbending and uptight about everything in their lives, but as it happens, practicing self-discipline can make you feel happier at times ahead in the future and also right in the very moment you are working and living in.

According to research published in psychological journals, self-control demonstrated that it is more a mindset of managing conflicting achievements, or goals, and not about deprivation or punishment. There is the association that disciplined people happen to be more task-oriented and are therefore less capable of living in the moment and having a ball. The studies conducted to measure the levels of happiness in highly disciplined people had some interesting results.

Life satisfaction and self-discipline were strongly correlated in surveys and studies compiled using a variety of participants, asking questions relating to mood, desires, goals, and ambitions. The research seemed to indicate that this correlation had everything to do with the relationship between feeling good for your achievements, and bad when you lost focus and left your goals out to dry, relating self-discipline and control to the consequences of satisfaction for meeting goals.

The research also demonstrated how self-discipline could improve the mood at the moment. Participants who answered in favor of feeling relatively happier and experiencing fewer bad moods, were more self-controlled in general, on account of exposing themselves to fewer challenges or situations that would cause them personal setbacks in the first place. Essentially, the study showed that self-disciplined people feel happier because they avoid creating conflict for themselves.

How then do we associate being more self-disciplined with a miserly, Puritanical character or quality of life? Let's take dieting as an example. Dieting is about self-control and can often lead less to happy thoughts and more to thoughts of stress or anxiety. Usually, this occurs as a relationship with a lack of wanting to avoid something and a decision to accept temptation, creating that inner conflict with the self. Exercising self-discipline can feel taxing at times when you are just learning these new skills. This comes from a pattern of seeing self-discipline as difficult and hard to do, rather than focusing on the rewards and the results. But the proof of happiness is in the cake you bake.

When you prove to yourself that you can do something, you show yourself how much you value your journey and your accomplishments. A self-discipline is an act of self-love, and when you are giving yourself what you want and need in order to live a full life, you can create that sense of inner abundance and wealth that matches your goal of outer abundance and wealth.

Self-discipline doesn't have to be challenging or uncomfortable. It can actually be a very enlivening and joyful experience because of how it can make you feel when you accomplish something. Little acts of self-discipline lead to large feelings of self-confidence. Whatever your goal may be, it will show you how important it is to treat yourself in the way that you know you deserve to be treated by YOU.

Discipline coming from outside of yourself, for example, a parent, partner, or colleague, can feel a lot different. It can feel difficult, more challenging, and often unwanted and seen as a cause of insecurity or self-doubt. Supporting yourself from within with your own self-discipline practices is a better pathway to understanding how to become the you that you want to be and already are.

People all over the world are hard at work to accomplish something. Not everyone has the self-discipline to do it, and they get burned out, self-deprecating, unhappy, and make it a lot harder of a job than it needs to be. Focusing on the fuel of persistence and the consistency of your actions towards your goals leads to good habits that become a part of who you are and how you make your life work.

You are the key to your success and happiness, and all you have to do is teach yourself how to stay on track with a positive attitude and feel the happiness that comes from living as a self-disciplined person on the road to success.

As human beings and as inherently social creatures, we share a lot with each other even when we don't intend to or realize we're sharing. We pass information from person to person every day. One of the things we share the most are our emotions.

Of course, you'd choose happiness—who wants to feel anger, rage, sadness or regret? When you cultivate happiness within yourself, it can begin as if you were holding a single candle. The wind is going to test that flame, and even put it out sometimes. With practice, however, you can relight it. With even more practice, your candle becomes a lantern, protected from the wind, impossible to snuff out.

Your happiness can be like that, too. Angry people may come and go, but your inner fire burns on, and in doing so, draws people to it. That is the power of charisma.

Learn to Appreciate Yourself

A cornerstone of inner happiness is the skill of self-appreciation. You can get a head start on this important skill by setting time aside to make a list. Write down three to five things about yourself that you feel good about. Savor the positive emotions that come with recognizing these things.

Now, elaborate on this list by seeing if you can connect anyone else to these skills, traits, or achievements. Perhaps it was a parent or sibling, or foreman at a job site. Perhaps it was a professor in college, or an empathic coworker. Perhaps it was a best friend of two decades. Who contributed to the "you" you are today? Take time to relish the gratitude that comes from knowing those people helped you pave the way to the happiness of today.

Often, when we work on instilling happiness within ourselves and are practicing self-reflection, we also dig up painful or unpleasant memories or emotions. It's okay to think about these, as long as you're not going to let them linger. Rumination is the act of dwelling in the past, looking for places to lay blame for things going wrong; we often blame ourselves when we ruminate. Make the conscious decision to abandon this practice, in favor of gratitude and happiness. Building a powerful, confident self includes discarding that which hurts and undermines us.

Another good practice is at the end of each day, take time to consider the moments that were satisfying in some way, or that brought you happiness. If you found there weren't many of these, resolve to seek more happy moments tomorrow. Become an active participant in your daily life, seeking happiness, then taking the time to savor it once you find it.

Keeping a journal is a great way to be able to look back and realize you've had more good days than bad. In fact, decide today to stop labeling days as "bad"; unless a day is truly catastrophic, most days we consider "bad" were just full of obstacles and challenges. If we have enough self-belief and inherent joy within us, however, we can ride out those days without allowing them to get us down.

Work hard = be successful = be happy

But this formula is flawed and broken. For every time we achieve success, we then move the goalposts and expect happiness to be on the other side of that. So effectively we are always chasing happiness and never feel fulfilled.

Find Your Inner Happiness

We all have something that makes us move forward, that animates us, gives us strength and serves as propelling energy for our actions. It can be family, love, success, faith, a hobby, travel, etc. Whatever causes you this sensation, enjoy it. Cultivate this daily within you and cling to what keeps you walking. Put a reminder or symbol that refers to what makes you happy in one place you can see daily, not to forget and stay inspired.

Chapter 8. Understanding the Difference Between Mental Toughness and Resilience

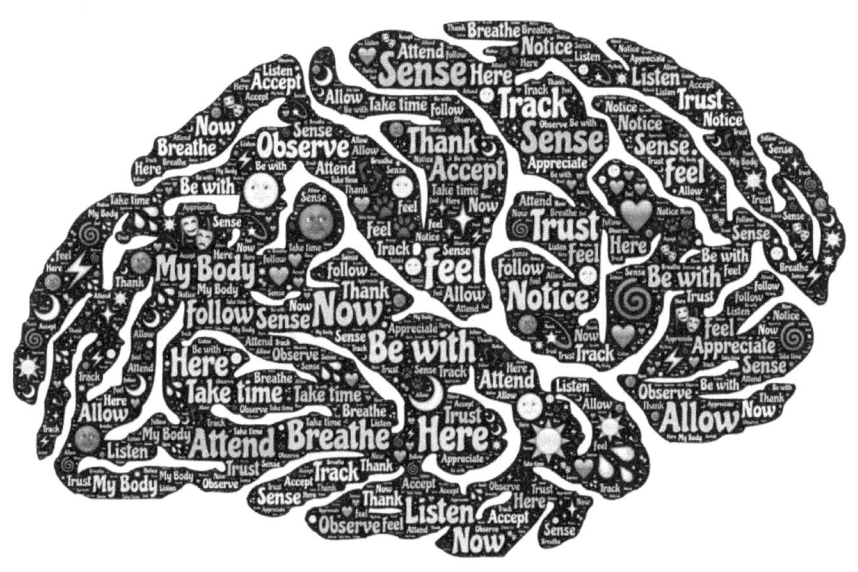

Due to their similarities, many people assume that mental toughness and resilience can be used interchangeably. However, according to Doug Strycharczyk, one of the pioneer researchers that tackled the concept of mental toughness, there are some important distinctions between the two concepts.

If you will recall from the first part, mental toughness or mental strength is defined as a person's ability to perform well despite facing obstacles, rejections, or adversities. Rather than regard a challenge as a threat, mentally strong individuals see them as an opportunity to become even better. Their approach in life can be best described as proactive and confident.

In comparison, resilience, in the field of psychology, refers to the ability to adapt to a highly stressful, traumatic, or turbulent situations. It can be observed whenever someone manages to pick himself up, and then continue to rise above the situation.

To be considered a mentally tough person, you must exhibit resilience to some degree. However, the leading experts on this matter explain that being resilient does not automatically make someone mentally tough. Given this, Strycharczyk suggested that mental toughness can be equated with "prosperity", while resilience can be thought of as "survival".

Take a look at the stories of two girls whose accounts of the same incident show the subtle differences between mental toughness and resilience.

When they were only fifteen years old, twins Zoey and Lulu lost their parents in a tragic car accident. Each of them mourned for a significant amount of time, but through their own will and with the help of other family members and their close friends, both girls managed to get themselves out of their grieving period, albeit in different ways.

Zoey's path diverged from Lulu's when the latter decided to take up a new hobby—dancing—while her sister started resuming her interest in painting. The people around them observed how Lulu poured her energy and time on her daily dance practices. On the other hand, Zoey took a more deliberate pace by going to the art galleries that she and their parents enjoyed visiting.

As she continued to spend time by browsing through art, Zoey was reminded of her reasons for taking up painting in the first place. This prompted her to pick up the paintbrush again, and to begin expressing her grief through her artworks. Though the theme has changed from before, her loved ones were relieved to see her going back to how things were before the accident.

Lulu, to her credit, also had a cathartic moment when she realized her passion for dance. It took her mind away from the pain of losing her parents, thus allowing her to discover new aspects of herself. Though she still missed her parents a lot, she figured that the best way to honor their memory is by making the most out of the life they have given her. With this conviction, Lulu set out a goal for herself: earn a dance scholarship from a prestigious performance arts school.

Looking at Zoey's successful attempt to bounce back from her grief, her side of the story shows more characteristics associated with resilience. Lulu, on the other hand, turned her grief as an opportunity to draw out of herself something new and better—which may be considered as a sign that she is becoming mentally stronger.

Neither of their reactions is inherently better than the other's. They have gotten over the traumatic phase of their lives and came out of it with the desire to keep moving forward. The trajectory from here on would likely be different for the sisters, but that does not mean that Zoey would never exhibit mental toughness like her sister, and that Lulu would never experience a moment of resilience at any point in her future.

Ultimately, what the twins' story suggests is that even though resilience and mental toughness are different from one another, each serves a purpose, and can be highly beneficial for anyone who needs to get back on their feet after going through harrowing experiences.

In addition, you should also keep in mind that the two concepts are not mutually exclusive from one another. Like the girls, you may have to become resilient or mentally tough, depending on what the circumstances and your current situation calls for.

You have already learned in some segments about the various ways on how you can improve your mental toughness. Now, you must discover how you can become a resilient person.

Much like mental strength, resilience is not something that everyone has upon birth. Instead, it is something that is gained and can be improved upon throughout a person's life. To guide you through the process of building up your resilience, here are the top 10 strategies that have been proven to effective by the experts:

1. Learn from your past.

By exploring your past experiences, you will be able to form a more comprehensive and effective plan for your development as a resilient person. To begin, you must examine yourself through the aid of the guide questions below:

- What events in your past have caused the highest amount of stress to you?
- How did each event affect you?
- Did you find the thought of your loved ones as helpful in getting you through your times of great need?
- Did you reach out to anyone for support? If yes, who?
- Did you learn anything about yourself or about your interactions with that person while he was supporting you? Specify what you have learned, if any.
- Did supporting others with similar problems as you do help you in overcoming your own suffering?
- What caused you to become more optimistic and hopeful during those times?

Write down your responses to these questions, preferably in a journal so you could easily look back at them in the future. Highlight the common themes among your answers. Reflect upon the results of your self-examination and use this as basis for your other strategies to develop mental resilience.

2. Stop thinking of your bad experiences in life as insurmountable blocks.

You cannot change everything around you to suit your preferences and needs. What you can change, however, is your own attitude and reaction towards the things that have caused you trouble, stress, pain, or trauma.

Furthermore, whenever you come across a stumbling block, remember to look beyond this obstacle because you may be able to see another way to get through it.

3. Become more accepting of the changes in your life.

Your current situation will not hold on forever. It may take a turn either for the better or for the worse. Regardless of the direction, the important thing is for you to learn how to accept the fact that change is constant, and that in most cases, there is nothing you can do to prevent it from happening. Given this, the right thing to do is to spend your time and effort on something else that is within your control.

4. Strengthen your connections to your social circles.

The people who care about you can help you enhance further your growing sense of resilience. Even if they do not show their support right now, they can still provide you with an environment wherein you would feel heard, understood, and loved.

These circles are not only limited to your family and friends. You can also reach out and strengthen your ties to your community as well.

5. Create and pursue SMART goals.

Though lofty goals may sound inspiring, it is still better to follow the SMART (specific, measurable, achievable, realistic, and timely) goal-setting technique when developing your resilience. Big, audacious goals can be your ultimate destination. But, to learn how to keep going despite any setback, you need to set smaller goals that will serve as signposts for the progress you have made so far.

To set SMART goals, just simply answer the following guide questions:

- In specific terms, what do you want achieved?
- How will you know if you have attained your goal?
- Is it within your capability and control?
- Realistically speaking, do you have a chance of accomplishing it?
- When exactly do you have to attain it?

For your reference, here is an example of a goal that meets the requirements of the SMART goal-setting technique: "I want to read this volume about mental toughness from cover to cover by month-end."

6. Consider your bad experiences as opportunities and lessons of self-discovery and self-improvement.

In most cases, a person would be able to gain a lot of insights about themselves and how the world works, in general - during and after experiencing an intensely difficult situation. If you would take the time to consider these as important life lessons, you will have an easier time looking for and identifying the opportunities for personal growth that they might be offering to you.

Studies show that people who have adapted this kind of thinking have noticed that their appreciation for the people and things in their life have significantly increased. Others also reported becoming more in touch with their spirituality as a result of the experience. There are also some who believe that the tragedies and trauma they have gone through improved and strengthened their relationships with the people who had gone through the same experience.

7. Improve your view about your self-worth.

Believing in your skills and capabilities could help promote your growth as a resilient individual. Without this, you might not trust yourself well enough to follow your own plans and instinct when the situation calls for it.

There are also plenty of other benefits for having confidence in yourself, aside from being able to think and function well even during stressful situations. According to multiple research studies, the following are the common benefits that you may expect just by having a good self-worth and self-confidence:

- Improved ability to convince and influence other people
- Reduced doubts, worries, and other negative thoughts
- Increased willpower and energy
- Higher satisfaction and happiness
- Enhanced leadership abilities
- More positive outlook in life
- Better communication and interpersonal skills

In order to improve your self-worth and confidence levels, you may start by identifying and accepting the good qualities and skills that you currently possess. Feel free to ask for the input of the people close to you as well since they likely have good perceptions about your strengths and good traits.

Experts also suggest setting and stacking smaller goals so that the positive effects of goal achievement can contribute to your development as a confident person.

Keeping your sights on these goals rather than perfection also helps in bringing up your self-worth and protecting yourself from being needlessly disappointed in yourself due to unreasonably high standards.

8. Remain optimistic.

Focusing on the negativity and your troubles would prevent you from finding an effective solution that will get you out of a bad situation. Maintaining a hopeful and positive outlook, on the other hand, can keep you going despite how the situation made you feel. It allows you to focus on the possibility that you will get over this challenge in your life, while also boosting your chances of actually coming up with a good solution to your problem.

According to studies, one of the best ways to remain optimistic despite experiencing a tragedy or a trauma is through visualization. By imagining yourself in a better position and more positive environment, you will be able to instill the right outlook and attitude within you. Furthermore, visualization has been proven quite effective in promoting goal achievement, thus further helping you get out of the bad situation you are currently in.

9. Practice self-care and self-compassion.

Extending kindness and care to yourself is an important factor in developing your resiliency. Otherwise, you would find it even harder to bounce back from difficult situations when your body and mind are not in good condition.

Self-care involves any kind of activity that improves your mood, while also lowering your stress and anxiety. Common examples of self-care initiatives include:

- Developing and following a good sleeping schedule
- Writing down your thoughts and feelings in a journal
- Catching up with a close friend or family member
- Doing mindful yoga
- Getting a relaxing massage
- Availing of your sick leave when necessary
- Exercising your body and mind regularly.

On the other hand, self-compassion refers to your ability to be kind to yourself even when you think that your current bad situation is due to your inadequacy, mistake, or failure. Much like self-care, it is a powerful tool against anxiety, as well as depression. You can enhance your self-compassion by:

- Practicing mindfulness

- Allowing yourself to be imperfect

- Spending your time by engaging in your hobbies and other interests

- Accepting your flaws as a person, and the mistakes you have made

- Refraining from making quick assumptions or baseless judgments about yourself

10. Learn and develop healthy habits.

Having the right set of habits can help you achieve your personal goals. This applies as well when it comes to building resiliency. If your day to day life consists of habits that promote good health and sound mind, then you will be able to concentrate more on dealing with the challenges that you might encounter.

Below are the top habits that could aid your development as a resilient individual:

- Eating six small meals throughout the day
- Refraining from eating junk food, sugary beverages, and alcohol
- Exercising the body at least every other day
- Planning in advance your activities and priorities
- Taking a walk around the park every afternoon

In case any of these habits are not part of your current routine, you may add them by going through the standard 4-stage habit creation process, or by stacking them with the good habits that you currently have.

Aiming to develop mental toughness does not mean that you should ignore your opportunities to build your resiliency. Each psychological concept may prove to be important in different moments of your life. Why limit yourself to only one when you have the chance and the means to become a well-rounded and well-prepared person.

Resilience is often discovered and tested only when the tragedy or trauma has already happened. You do not have to wait for such instances in your life to begin enhancing this quality within you. Start building your resiliency now so that you will be more prepared to handle the great adversities and hardships that might occur in the future.

Chapter 9. The Pitfalls of Improving Self-Discipline

Discipline is by far the most important virtue. After all, every single other virtue relies on a strong discipline. That being said, in the process of developing any quality or skill, there are certain risks associated with it.

Jealousy

As a direct result of becoming more disciplined, your accomplishments will be more impressive. Some of the people around you are likely to feel personally threatened by your success. It's not their higher self that is threatened; it is their identity. After all, if you are able to do so much, what does this say about them?

When you are close to someone, your identities will make an agreement behind your backs. They will decide to coordinate efforts to make sure that both of you don't change. However, when you are improving your discipline, you will experience some of the greatest changes in your life. If the people close to you are weak and are controlled by their identity, they may lash out at you when they see you becoming a better version of yourself. This might manifest itself in blunt "you have changed" comments, or it may show with more subtle jabs at your newfound success. These sorts of comments or actions are particularly dangerous because their identity isn't the only force trying to hold you back; your identity is trying to do exactly the same thing. Their identity is using whatever methods it can to try to give your identity the fuel it needs to retake control.

When you hear these sorts of comments laugh them off. If they make you angry use that as fuel to become more disciplined. If they make you question what you are doing, remember that their comments don't come from genuine concern, but rather they come from a place of insecurity. In some cases, their jealousy will cause them to somehow try to sabotage your success in more sinister ways. For example, a boss or a coworker who tries to prevent you from getting a promotion. Or a friend who attempts to sabotage your marriage. Because you don't necessarily know who will be offended by your success and who will lash out, it is best to remain humble and downplay your accomplishments whenever possible. Naturally, if you are trying to sell something or are running a business, it is a good idea to talk about what you are doing at every opportunity. But make sure to intersperse your sales pitch with a self-deprecating comment or two. Not everyone is controlled by their identity, in fact, many people will be overjoyed by your new zest for life. They will encourage you; they will push you to the next level, and they will want some of what you have made for yourself. Always remember who celebrates your success; these people should be treasured.

Perfectionism

There is a feedback loop between self-discipline and trying to be the best version of yourself you can possibly be. As your discipline increases, you will need to seek out new challenges to stretch your abilities; this means that you are constantly looking for ways to improve yourself. In order to continue to stretch your abilities your self-discipline will need to improve in order to compensate. If you can enter into this feedback loop, you will be able to rapidly transform your life. This transformation is generally positive, but the side effects can be a certain amount of neurotic perfectionism.

This volume stresses a very general broad idea of discipline, meaning that there are a number of different ways you can improve yourself. Having so many things you can do to make your life better should make you feel optimistic, however, some of the time you may feel overwhelmed by all of the different parts of your life you will eventually need to work on.

People respond to perfectionism in three different ways.

First, some people will try to do everything at once. They will want to improve their fitness, their career, their diet, their courage/vulnerability, their education, and start meditating all at the same time. If you try to do this, you will probably only stand for a short period of time before your motivation disappears and you revert to the same habits you had in the beginning or possibly even degenerate below your baseline.

The second typical response to perfectionism is to do nothing at all. You may feel like you will never be able to improve all of these different aspects of your life, so you don't end up improving any of them. This is a form of "paralysis by analysis."

Find one or two aspects of your life, which need to be improved, create a plan to go around anywhere from two to twelve weeks, execute your plan. After you have followed through with your program, reevaluate, and create another plan.

Losing Flexibility

In recent decades the bodybuilding and powerlifting community has learned to embrace the importance of stretching and other mobility-based exercises. Muscle-bound beasts like Kelly Starrett have been able to earn a comfortable living teaching lifter how to increase their range of motion. This is in stark contrast to the "17 exercises for giant triceps" approach.

Why are gym rats suddenly so focused on mobility? The answer is actually fairly self-evident. If you move a muscle through a range of motion for years, particularly if it is a partial range of motion, you lose flexibility in that joint over time.

So, if you go into the gym and push heavy iron day in and day out without stretching you will become more and more immobile. Bodybuilders don't have to move like ballerinas, but the gradual loss of range of motion from resistance exercises can limit the sorts of exercises which they can perform, and, in some cases, it can result in pain or injury.

Fortunately, for serious lifters, it turns out that it is actually fairly easy to maintain and improve flexibility by performing certain mobility exercises every day. Note: the problem is not that the lifters are too strong or too muscular; there are plenty of examples of very strong muscular people who are also totally mobile and healthy. Instead, the joint problems emerge in the process of developing muscularity and strength. This distinction is important when we draw our connection back to discipline.

Discipline has a lot of the same properties as a muscle. And if you use it every single day without stretching, it can become tight and immobile.

There are two implications of this analogy. One of them is literal, and the other is figurative. However, both of these implications are important for someone who is putting in a strong effort into developing their discipline.

The first, more literal implication, is that in the process of becoming disciplined, there is a tendency to become too structured and orderly losing one's ability to adapt in the process. Fortunately, it is possible to become extremely disciplined while maintaining your adaptability at the same time.

One strategy for maintaining adaptability is to dedicate some period of the day to free time. This doesn't have to be purely recreational time; however, it shouldn't be dedicated to any particular activity. You could spend this time reading, writing, or working on projects which you normally wouldn't have the time to get around to doing.

Another technique you can use to maintain your flexibility is to push yourself and try to do something which you aren't sure you can actually complete. This will have the added benefit of testing the limits of your discipline. Many people drastically underestimate their capacity for discipline until they actually test it.

The second more figurative loss of flexibility is a loss of spirit. You don't want to lose your playfulness in the process of developing your unshakeable resolve. It is important to remain goofy, silly, and to remember to smile.

Chapter 10. The Difference between Self-Discipline and Self-Control

When you need to stop one habit and start another one, it involves different psychological decisions. For instance, when you decide that you will stop taking any junk and that you will start eating healthy. The first decision is purely based on self-control, and the latter is all about self-discipline. It is important to know that the two are different. In that when you are successful in one, it does not guarantee success on the other one. The two might seem related, but they are different processes.

Self-control is mostly defined as when a person is able to control their pleasures, especially the emotional ones. The first urge that you get is controlled and stopped. You are able to make a decision to stop the urge to do something. Like when you get home from work, and you are tired. When you are triggered, you can get angry very fast. So, to exercise self-control, you need to avoid falling for the triggers.

When your child provokes you, you should be able to control the urge to scream at them. Also, avoid having to exchange words with your spouse. Keep it cool and look for something that might distract you. Self-discipline can be explained as self-control that s normally observed over a longer time. For instance, you control all the negative effects that you have, by ensuring that you work on them for on a set time period. With tine, self-discipline can be considered a behavior.

Most people believe that the two are related. They may seem so, but in the real sense, there is some difference. Their implications and effect are considered different. So, after this, ensure you can comfortably differentiate the two. When you use a dictionary to define the two, you will likely find that the two are related.

However, psychologically, these two are different. They involve different processes. The difference is mainly in, self-discipline is more of yes, good, go, and keep going. Self-control is about saying no; you need to stop. Self-control is a habit that s triggered by environment influence or peer pressure. It involves the desire or urges to start a habit. It also involves the delay of sense gratification. It will bring about the battle for emotional desires and intellectual knowledge. You'll need to make a decision on either psychological and physical pleasure or believing that something better will come up in the future.

Most people do not understand what self-discipline is, and this ends up bringing up a lot of misconceptions. Many people believe that you need to be too controlling in order to be considered to have self-discipline. You should be very strict about how you live and how you relate to other people. For example, if you are on a strict diet, you should always be at home. In order to have more concentration, that is indeed not true. That is actually the opposite of what self-discipline is all about. The main reason behind self-discipline is to ensure that there are changes in your life—changes that will have an effect on your body and mind. And changes that will help you become a better and positive person. You will have your plans set in, and then you will have the pressure to accomplish all that. The better the hard work and consistency you put in the better the results and performance. This will help with the transformation. Do not think that with the willpower that you have, it is a guarantee for excellence. Willpower is considered a resource to help you. But do not base your energy and efforts there. This is because it might fail you, and this will discourage you.

When you are self-disciplined most of the time, you have a plan and the steps to accomplish it. So, you'll have fewer struggles when it comes to accomplishing what you desire, and you will be able to do that with less pressure. When you are under pressure to do a lot and what you intend to accomplish is not of interest. Then the probability of failing is very high. And self-discipline can also be defined as when a person is willing to fail when they are under pressure.

And self-control, on the other hand, it when you have the capability of not failing. When you want to stop a bad habit and your intentions s to stick to that. Which in many scenarios, it's not possible? They will give up when they experience the problem again, and they will not bother in doing anything about it. And the effect of not doing anything is you'll be overtaken by negative effects which will in return affect your plans and life. And why it is the opposite of self-discipline is that that situation will bring no pressure or the urge that you need to change.

It is important to avoid the option to fail, avoid making the same mistake over and over again. Since if you've been doing the same thing and you keep on failing. It is high time to make a change. It is advisable to try different things, new things. You can start by looking at what the other people are doing, and if you believe they are good; it is a good thing to try out.

When you have an activity that you've already been doing, for self-control you will have to stop that. You will get the urge to stop either after you start, or you'll have a hard time deciding if you should do it. As for self-discipline, you will start a new habit or project, and you'll make sure you stick with it. In short, the difference between is one requires you to stop doing or thinking about it, and the latter involves starting and enjoying the benefits.

Another example can be when you have taken your first snack, and then you have the urge to pick a second one. Self-control is applicable when you stop the urge to eat the second snack. And self-discipline will come in when we overcome the urge to pick another snack next time. Self-control is all about fighting the habits that you want to stop and sticking to that decision. You'll be able to overcome any desire to get involved in any habits that have emotional and physical effects.

Self-discipline is the influence that will motivate us to wake up when the alarm goes off. While self-control, on the other hand, will make us overcome the temptation to snooze the alarm. When you do not feel like doing anything, self-discipline will motivate you to do something. You will be expected to be consistent, and you will plan exactly what needs to be done. You'll be motivated to work within reasonable set deadlines in order to be productive and responsible for our choices and decisions. Self-discipline is all about the long-term goals, while self-control is all about the short-term goals.

When we lack self-control, we will not have the discipline to do what we had planned, and it will affect us with such choices. And again, when we lack self-discipline, we are not in a better position to exercise self-control, this is because on not being consistent and we are not controlled by a habit to keep us in check. Self-discipline does not work on a level that is primal like self-control. Self-control actions will involve short term pleasures like when you smoke, take alcohol, and when you eat something. On the other hand, self-discipline is applicable at a higher level. It involves several effects like being successful, having the hopes to prosper, future plans, and the urge to accomplish something. For instance, when you look forward to reporting to work on time, passing your exams, academic excellence, and adhering to rules and regulations at work.

The effect will be to forget about our current plans and only concentrate on what we want in the future. You'll always believe that the future plans are the ones that are better, and your full concentration should be there. You will decide on the long-term plans that you want to accomplish, and you will have the motivation to stick on them. If for instance, it is in business, you will ensure you put in some extra hours and to increase your income. When you are in school, you will be motivated to work extra hard to pass that exam and graduate, and it is at your workplace, the more hours you put in, the higher the production rate.

When you lack you lack self-control, your efforts to succeed in your plans will be thwarted. For example, when you do not overcome the urge to get a new car. This decision will have you up in more expenses like maintenance fees, fueling, and this might end up piling on your debts. You should also know that, when you have self-discipline in excess, it can affect your self-control. And the effects will be being too tough and not social at all.

You need to know how to plan, balance, and be in moderation. There are basic elements when it comes to self-discipline and self-control. When all that is observed, you will be able to control all your urges, manage all the effects, and then enjoy all the benefits. You need to critically analyze and know the areas that self-control will be applicable. The most common areas when self-control is needed the most is in financial management and weight problems.

Always ensure that the plans and expectations that you have are realistic. This will help in ensuring that they are easily attainable. You will have less stress when it comes to executing the duties to accomplish them.

Make a plan on what you will need to accomplish and at what timeframe. Realistic goals go hand in hand with realistic timeframes. Have specific plans on what areas you will want to accomplish and stick to the plan.

Break down your plans in smaller steps and have a plan between each accomplished step and the final major plan. Like when you are into junk, and you're planning to stop. You can start with smaller portions before deciding to stop. Do not have thoughts and think that you have failed, when you have unrealistic plans and goals that will be the issue. Plan on something that you are passionate about, and you'll surely succeed in that.

When you have problems that you believe you should give more attention, like drug usage and alcohol consumption. You will need to seek professional help. You should think of it as a sign that you are strong not as a weakness. This is a brave step to admit that you are troubled, and you need help. Always work hard to have self-discipline; this skill has numerous skills that will help in your life. You will get help to deal with your relationship, your family, at your workplace, with friends, and even in your academics. Always think of the places that will need more self-discipline and those that will need more self-control. When you fail, it might be harsh. Not many people are comfortable with being a failure.

What you should know is that, when you are looking for a habit or skill to help you with faster success. Then self-discipline will. On the other hand, self-control is normally used when you are in a situation that requires an immediate response. The main purpose is to avoid immediate gratification and any validation. When you set your mind towards immediate gratification, it will do you harm. The best thing to do is to correct that urge immediately to avoid any effects in the future.

And self-discipline is the consistent habit that one has in order to accomplish a goal. Always pushing forward, beg focused, and determined that all will turn out to be successful. The main difference is that self-control is normally used when there is a need or a situation to be reactive. And self-discipline is a consistent habit, that is applied daily for a longer time. Self-discipline is all about being focused and the motivation to push through. Even when you lack interest, you have the zeal to push through—the constant motivation to carry on and know that you'll succeed. So, at this point, it is obvious that the two are important in your life. So, you need to think about which one applies more in your life and make an informed decision.

Chapter 11. Self-Discipline, Confidence and Motivation

Self-discipline is a key component in your attempt to achieve any worthy goal. However, note that its benefits are not limited to that. It is also a major help in boosting your confidence. Basically, self-discipline is all about giving yourself valid reasons to do certain things and stick to certain habits for a long time. Of course, this boils down to developing internal motivation and the desire to achieve your ultimate goal, but more than being a process of chasing after a goal, it also involves your ability to take full control of your impulses and desires. It requires you to maintain your focus in order for you to be successful in reaching your ultimate goal. It requires you to develop certain habits that aid in attaining your desired goal, outcome or objective. That said, you need to take small yet consistent actions that can help develop the necessary habits. Note, however, that developing self-discipline is not only about doing something on a consistent basis. It is actually more on consistently correcting and controlling your behaviors, so as to make it easier for you to adapt to all the changing scenarios and conditions.

It also requires you to train yourself proactively to abide by certain rules and live up to specific standards, making it easier for you to align and shape your behaviors and thoughts to your intended goals and tasks. Cultivating self-discipline, therefore, is crucial to your success. Aside from boosting your productivity since it significantly improves your focus, it also tends to strengthen and enhance your confidence.

You can feel your confidence improving while practicing and cultivating self-discipline, especially once you notice how you improved your sense of control when doing your projects and tasks. You are confident that nothing will distract or sidetrack you. With a higher level of confidence and self-discipline, you also subsequently build your tolerance and allow yourself to get a lot of things done with the least amount of time and effort. To get in the self-disciplined mindset while boosting your self-confidence at the same time, here are some tips that you can easily implement:

Create a supportive environment

Your confidence in your ability to develop self-discipline will most likely dwindle if you are not in a supportive environment. You have to constantly be in a kind of environment, which supports the self-discipline mindset. If your environment lacks your needed support, then expect to always find friction, which will eventually cause you to struggle in developing both the confidence and discipline that you need to attain your desired outcome.

That said, it is necessary to create a working environment, which supports your goal, as well as the habits and actions that you intend to execute on a daily basis. To help you develop a more supportive environment, you need to consider several factors, including the following:

☐ Rituals and habits that you need to do to attain your goal

☐ Actions that you need to consistently do

☐ Ability of your present environment to support the needed actions and habits

☐ Changes that you need to make to create a supportive environment

Your goal, therefore, is to create a work environment, which motivates you to execute the actions and habits that you need to implement each day. You need an environment, which will inspire you and commit to attaining your goal over the long haul.

Groom yourself

There are times when it takes a lot of self-discipline to practice the right grooming and hygienic practices every day. However, note that making it a habit to groom yourself is one of the easiest ways to practice discipline while also boosting your confidence. A regular shower and shave, for instance, can make you feel good, thereby raising your confidence, which is good for your self-image. It also has the tendency to improve your mood.

You also have to dress nicely. Dressing up nicely can make you feel better about yourself, plus knowing that you look good can further heighten your desire to do things correctly. You will feel more presentable and successful. Proper grooming plus dressing up nicely can also make you feel like you're ready to tackle all the challenges that you'll face.

This does not mean, however, that you should splurge too much on expensive clothes and beauty products. All it takes is to fill your closet and your beauty arsenal with products that look good on you, regardless of their prices. Even if you're wearing an inexpensive outfit, if it looks good on you and suits you, you will instantly feel confident and more motivated to tackle everything that you set yourself out to do.

Think and act positively

Your confidence and self-discipline will most likely dwindle if you constantly feel your mind with negative thoughts. Make sure to practice the habit of cultivating positivity within you. Replace your negative and distracting thoughts with more positive ones. To kill negative thoughts and behaviors, it helps to raise your awareness about your self-talk. This actually refers to your thoughts about your own self and the things that you do.

For instance, if you're disciplining yourself to exercise on a daily basis, then your mind may start countering you by saying that it's too hard. The problem is that when you let this thought overpower you, then there is a great possibility that you will be unable to follow through with your regular exercise routines. You may stop exercising and do something more convenient and entertaining, instead – like watching TV.

In this case, it pays to recognize your own thoughts, so you can instantly detect when you're already doing the negative self-talk. The good thing about recognizing your negative thoughts is that you can easily stomp on them and kill them before they damage your confidence and your discipline to do things. You can also immediately replace them with positive ones that are guaranteed to help you improve.

Get to know more about yourself

When planning to raise your confidence and cultivate discipline, it helps to know exactly who you are. Note that in some cases, your enemy is your own self, and you have the chance to beat it if you know exactly who you are (as an enemy). It would be hard to beat your enemy if you don't know him. In this case, it helps to overcome your negative self-image, so you can start replacing it with more positivity and higher level of confidence.

One tip to get to know yourself even better is to listen to your own thoughts. Write anything about yourself in the journal. It's also advisable to write your thoughts about yourself there. If you noticed that you have listed several negative thoughts about your own self, then it's time to analyze each one. Think about what prompts you to view yourself that way.

After the analysis, start thinking about the positive things about yourself. These should include everything that you like, and you can do well. Try to replace the negative ones with the positive things that you thought about yourself. So, the main goal of this tip is to begin by thinking about your weaknesses and limitations then analyzing whether these are real or just made up by your own mind. Dig deeper then embrace positivity, and you will surely come out having greater discipline and confidence.

Create a list of what you have achieved in the past

This is really helpful if you constantly lack the confidence and the discipline to move forward. By creating a list of your accomplishments in the past, you will start feeling good about yourself, and this can significantly boost your confidence and strengthen your resolve and discipline. Make sure to update this list often and post it in a place where you can always say it. Stop the urge to say that you haven't actually accomplished anything. Note that even minor successes matter here. No matter how minor the accomplishment is, write it down. Keep in mind that success is not only about career and wealth. It could be as minor as being able to cook a good recipe or bake a delicious cake, maintaining a good relationship with your family or being able to stick to healthy eating and workout habits. Seeing even your minor accomplishments is actually uplifting and inspiring – a big help in cultivating both your self-discipline and self-confidence.

Increase your skills and competence

Improving your skills and competence through continuous education is really a huge help in honing self-discipline and raising your confidence. Even minor steps to improving your confidence can help. For instance, if your goal is to become a more competent writer, then avoid tackling the whole writing profession at once. What you have to do is to discipline yourself to practice more. You can do so by writing on a daily basis.

Discipline yourself to allot a specific portion of your time each day to write. You can do journaling, blogging, short story writing, or taking in some freelance writing tasks. If you write consistently, then you'll notice a significant improvement in your skills. Even thirty minutes a day practicing your craft is already a big help in raising your skills and competence. An advantage of setting this kind of habit is that it helps you become more disciplined, plus it can significantly boost your confidence, knowing that you're getting better and better each day.

Inner drive and motivation are also one of the aspects of your life where self-discipline plays a vital role. If you have self-discipline, then it will also be easier for you to motivate and drive yourself to do something. Self-discipline and motivation actually work hand in hand. Your initial inspiration is actually your motivation. However, when you lose it, your self-discipline will help keep you moving forward.

To ensure that these two important aspects – self-discipline and motivation – work in your favor, it is important to practice the following tips on a regular basis. Most of them are designed to help boost your motivation while also retaining a high level of self-control and discipline.

Develop self-knowledge

Discipline involves taking action based on what you think is best for you without having to think about what you presently feel. Therefore, one of the first traits that you have to develop self-discipline, and eventually boosting your motivation, is self-knowledge. Decide on the specific behavior, which perfectly reflects your values and goals. This step actually requires effective self-analysis and introspection. This makes it necessary to put it down into writing.

It's advisable to spend time writing your ambitions, goals and dreams. If possible, write a personal mission statement, as well. Doing so will definitely help you understand yourself even better. It will show you who you are and what you value. This will let you develop self-knowledge, which is one of the keys to cultivating your desired level of self-discipline.

Create a plan and form habits

Note that the length of time it takes to form a specific habit actually depends from one person to another. Habit formation does not need to be too complex and automatic. It should be simple, realistic and doable. In this case, you need to develop a more concrete plan, so you will have an easier time sticking to your habits. Once good habits are formed, it will be harder for distractions and temptations to break down your resolve, discipline and motivation.

Set clear and specific goals

If you want to succeed in building motivation and discipline, then clarifying your goals and making them more specific is an important technique you need to implement. Make sure that you know exactly what you want. You also need clear reasons on why you want it. If you're unsure of what you want, then you will just have a difficult time attaining it. Your motivation and discipline will dwindle from one point to another. Motivate yourself by ensuring that you have a clear picture of your desired end result. Knowing the exact outcome, you intend to accomplish is very motivating, so disciplining yourself to take all the necessary actions to reach it will be easier. If you have a clear picture of your desired result in mind, then building up your motivation to reach it will easily come next.

Think long-term

To continuously motivate yourself, you have to develop the ability to think for the long term. This is a huge help in overcoming minor and major challenges that may come your way as you make your move towards your ultimate goal. Keep in mind that once you execute a long-term strategy, you will inevitably face hardships and challenges along the way. You can overcome all these by looking at your established long-term picture. Avoid waiting and procrastinating even further, as this can only make it harder for you to get past the challenges. Think about the end result – how it feels like to overcome the hard stuff and finally reach your goal. By allowing yourself to savor what you'll most likely feel as you reach your goal, it will be easier for you to push yourself forward.

Reassess and make the necessary adjustments

However, if you notice that you constantly hit the walls, instead of moving forward, then maybe it is the right time to assess the situation again. Analyze the situation and find out if it would help to implement an alternative course of action. If you constantly face the same challenge over and over again, then your motivation and discipline will eventually get ruined.

In this case, it helps to make some adjustments on your strategies. Find out if there are other more efficient ways to move towards your goal without facing the same challenges over and over again. Keep in mind that the key here is the end result. The road towards getting there actually has several directions. This means that just because you have already created a plan, you have to stick to it even if it is no longer working. Remember that there are other ways and solutions and you need to find the one, which perfectly works for you.

Create a mantra

Mantra is not only designed for yogis. It actually works for everyone – whether one is practicing yoga or not. Mantra actually refers to a verbal statement, which works effectively in reinforcing a more positive mindset. It is helpful in improving your motivation, cultivating discipline and uplifting you. Create a mantra, which really suits you and resonates with you.

Your mantra could be as simple as saying how strong you are and how capable you are to overcome all struggles and challenges. You may also use your creativity in creating more powerful mantras. Begin each morning of your day by saying the mantra aloud. Repeat it often. The more you repeat the mantra, the higher your chances of believing that it will really happen.

Build routines and rituals

Another thing that you can do to maintain a higher level of motivation plus ensuring that you stay disciplined for a long time is to set your own routines and rituals. The rituals should be inspiring enough, and these should be something that you can easily stick to every day. Your routines and rituals should also drive you to move forward and reach for your goal.

Be willing to conduct experiments on which routine and ritual will work for you. For instance, if you notice that a quick walk outside in the morning helps you clear your mind while also improving your perspective and mood all throughout the day, then you can make a habit out of it. Set around fifteen minutes each day taking that walk in the morning.

If you noticed how helpful reading at least a portion of a good manuscript is in giving you a more peaceful sleep, then make this activity a part of your daily routines. Find out which daily routines and rituals work for you. Just make sure that they stimulate happiness and peacefulness. Note that if you feel happier and more relaxed, then it will be easier for you to cultivate discipline and retaining a higher level of motivation.

Conquer your fears

Your fears can damage your motivation and discipline in an instant, so you have to look for ways to conquer them. Fear actually comes in all sizes and shapes. It could be fear of public speaking, failure, commitment, heights, etc. Find out which among your fears specifically prevents you from reaching for your goals. Remember that if you don't do something to face them, then you will most likely give up on your dreams and goals.

Face your fears, and you will notice how effective it is in giving you a strong sense of achievement, confidence and accomplishment. Conquering your fears also helps you broaden your horizon. It serves as your steppingstone towards attaining all your dreams and goals in life.

Commit to cultivating self-discipline

Self-discipline and motivation go hand in hand. That said, it is crucial to commit to cultivating self-discipline. Aside from writing down your values and goals, commit to them internally. If you don't, then you will just lose your enthusiasm to reach them. When your initial rush of enthusiasm fades, you will be at risk of struggling to complete what you've started.

If you have a hard time sticking to your commitments, then it's advisable to make a conscious decision to keep track of what you told yourself you will do. Constantly follow through on the time you said you will do it and the manner through which you'll do it. Keep track of all your commitments. Doing so can help you stick to them no matter what.

Chapter 12. Techniques to improve your mental toughness

Improving Focus With The Help Of Meditation And Visualization

meditation and visualization play a big role in improving focus. Political candidates, professional athletes, and even motivational speakers use this technique before their big performances to keep them calm and have clear goals.

Visualization through meditation attracts the outcomes you desire. It involves focusing on positive outcomes for the present regardless of your past glories or failures. Once you meditate and visualize your performance beforehand, you will be in a better position to play out your performance as you had already visualized it in your mind.

Enhancing Visualization To Improve Focus

Visualization through meditation is a concept that has been around for centuries. Monks and most recently yogis have been using this technique to enhance their mental, spiritual, emotional, and even physical states. Over the years, meditation has been used successfully to cure insomnia, depression, ADHD, and other mental problems.

Meditation also deepens the connection between one's body to their emotional and spiritual selves. This deeper connection between one's physical and non-physical state helps people become more in tune with them. It even gets better; meditation is a technique that can be used by people from all religions and belief systems.

If you have goals to achieve, you'll be glad to learn that successful figures, such as Tiger Woods, Oprah, and Arnold Schwarzenegger, all use visualization to achieve their goals.

In life, there are so many big decisions to make, such as the following: "Which career path should I take?" "Who can I fully place my trust in?" "Am I ready to take the next step in my life?" This final question especially can apply to so many aspects of life, such as when trying to know whether or not to get married, to have kids, pursue another college degree, start a business or get employed, etc.

Unfortunately, most people go with the flow when it comes to such important questions instead of making active decisions on them. Visualization through meditation sharpens up one's focus in life. It clears off the noise in your life and gives direction to your life. One thing in life is that if you don't visualize where you are heading, you will land anywhere. However, if your destination is clear, then you can easily navigate your way to reach your destination.

When it comes to achieving your goals, meditation is a three-step process that involves seeing your goal, believing in it, and repeating it in your mind. Meditation is a long-term process that entails a few minutes every day to master. Everyone has a unique way of meditating, and once you start the art, you can develop your own unique way of meditation.

Giving Your Best When Under Pressure

How does pressure feel like? Well, have you ever felt like suddenly everyone in your life is breathing down your neck to deliver on something and you feel that you can't take it anymore?

All adult people go through periods such as these when they are put under pressure by their family or friends in their personal lives at home, by their bosses who are pressuring them to complete projects before the deadline, or even by the school when a project is due or an examination is coming up.

These stressful situations can be so intense that one might be tempted to lose their bearing and burn bridges with their acquaintances or throw in the towel altogether.

Staying Motivated

Motivation is about finding the inspiration to accomplish what you set your heart and mind to do. The most meaningful goals are long-term accomplishments and require one to stay motivated throughout life's journey. Staying motivated is an important technique to learn if you are going to accomplish your goals. Ask yourself the following questions:

Are my goals meant to benefit just me, or will others benefit from them?

What value will be achieving the goals add to my life? How will my life change when pursuing these goals and after I have achieved my goals?

How will I feel after achieving my goals?

Unfortunately, when the journey is long, it is only human to lose some motivation along the way. However, there are ways that can help you bring back that motivation and inspiration when going through those tough periods.

The following are some ways:

1. Establishing the reason behind wanting to accomplish specific goals

2. This is a good way to keep motivated. If your reasons for pursuing a certain goal are based on self-interest alone, they hold less importance in your mind.

3. Accepting mistakes

4. The path to achieving goals is an unpredictable path and has many challenges. It is human to make mistakes, and instead of

beating yourself up for the mistakes, think of them as opportunities to learn and grow.

5. Break down your goal into smaller tasks

The brain is a complex human organ and is designed for viewing things in many dimensions. Accomplishing a goal can be complicated, but when you break down your goal into smaller tasks and set deadlines, you will be in a better position to finish the tasks individually and accomplish your goals. Smaller tasks are easier to accomplish and focusing on individual tasks will keep you motivated.

Developing Self-Control

Self-control is an important technique when pursuing goals. Unfortunately, most people are programmed to give more importance to instant gratification rather than going through challenges to accomplish their goals. Well, self-control is a quality that allows a person to override their emotional desire for instant results and persevere through pain and challenges to accomplish long-term goals.

When people practice self-control, they choose to ignore their primal feelings, impulses, and habits to achieve more important things. When you ignore such impulses, you are teaching your brain to derive more pleasure and satisfaction in achieving long-term goals.

Good intentions alone are not effective in developing a strong sense of self-control. You might want to lose weight, but you love eating unhealthy foods. Do you have the discipline to do what's necessary to lose weight, i.e., exercising and eating healthy foods? Self-control needs desire, dedication, and a plan to resist the temptation of falling back to negative habits.

Taking On Challenges And Responsibilities

Challenges and responsibilities come in various forms for different people, and the more you grow as a person, the more they present themselves in your life. One important saying that's been repeated to the point that it has become a cliché is "more money, more problems." Young people have minimum responsibilities and challenges and think that they will accomplish all their goals once they start earning.

One thing that they don't seem to realize is that as the money starts streaming in, the more their needs and wants to grow as well as the needs and wants of the people around them. Unpredictable events, such as illness, unemployment, divorce, and death, happen in their lives which destroy their plans.

Life is a constant force of change that leaves people reacting rather than approaching it actively. So, when you ask most people to take on more challenges and responsibilities, they will most probably turn the opportunity down as they already have their plates full of other commitments.

The challenges and responsibilities in your life at the present moment are there because you are equipped to handle them. When you shun away the opportunity to take on more responsibilities, you are shunning away a great opportunity to grow as an individual.

Embracing Positive Thinking

Most people dread Mondays. Others dread waking up early in the morning. When you think about these two scenarios logically, they don't make sense. Monday comes right after a weekend, and this is when one is expected to be full of energy and ready for work. The same principle applies in the morning. The morning is when you should feel invigorated from the night's sleep. There are also days where one rolls out of bed and immediately your mind tells you that it is going to be a difficult day. Such a negative reinforcement sets the tone for the day, and you find yourself experiencing a snowball effect of problems throughout the day.

One thing for sure is that you cannot expect to have a perfect day where everything goes your way. Reality dictates that some disappointments will come your way at some point during the day. However, this is not an excuse to live out your day in anticipation of disappointment. This is because the more you anticipate disappointment, the more you invite it into your life.

In addition, there is so much negativity going on in the world at the moment. Whenever you switch on your TV to watch the news or log into social media, you will find bad news everywhere. Sometimes, it is important to know what is going on around the world, but you should not have to carry the weight of saving the world single-handedly on your shoulders. Learn to stay away or block out negativity from your life.

Determination To Succeed

From the millions and possibly billions of people around the globe that made New Year's resolutions, have you ever wondered how many of these people followed up on their resolutions?

Distinguishing Between The Controllable And Uncontrollable

Young kids believe their parents have control over everything. As they grow a little older, they begin to believe that they run the world. This is reinforced when their parents get them anything, they wish for which gives them a false sense of control. Suddenly, when something doesn't go their way (as it should), they throw tantrums to show their anger.

Fast forward into adult life and the realization that their level of control is minimum and it will keep decreasing as they get older. The ability to distinguish between the controllable and uncontrollable is important.

The difference between the controllable and uncontrollable is small. There are things humans are capable of doing but have been outlawed because of various reasons. For instance, it is against the law for financial traders to manipulate the markets by insider trading as it gives them an unfair advantage over other traders in what should be a fair financial market.

Accepting That Competition Is Inevitable

Competition comes in various forms in our everyday lives. Whether it is in the business, workplace, and even sports, competition is rife, and everyone is scrambling to be the front-runner.

With this harsh reality, the critical questions are as follows: how should we respond to it? Should we embrace or run away from it?

There is no doubt that there are some days where we wish our competition would disappear so that we can deal with life more easily.

Bouncing Back From Setbacks

Setbacks are a natural part of life. It is important to equip yourself with coping mechanisms that will help you deal with setbacks. The more accustomed you get to dealing with setbacks, the more you can build up your resilience to keep moving forward despite the setbacks.

Constantly bouncing back from setbacks requires a great deal of resilience and persistence. Your resilience and persistence are the attributes that will keep you going after failure when the goings get hard and your motivation is drained. But how do you build up the resilience and persistence to give you the strength to bounce back from setbacks?

Developing Unshakable Self-Belief In Your Abilities To Succeed

Unshakable self-belief is critical when working toward your goals. Fortunately, for some people, this belief comes to them naturally. Unfortunately, for some people, they have self-esteem issues, and self-belief has to be learned through years of practice.

Self-belief can be described as the fuel or catalyst that accelerates people toward achieving success. One recipe for success is setting a clear goal and developing a stable belief in your ability to achieve the goal. If you have the determination, resilience, and perseverance to stick to your objectives until the end, then you can achieve everything you set your mind to. This recipe applies to everyone.

Acquiring The Necessary Skills Required To Accomplish Your Goal

Most people seek to excel in their jobs and take their careers to the next level, but today it's becoming extremely hard because different people have their own unique talents which, therefore, result in tough competitions. The best way to stay ahead of your game in your workplace and in the industry is by developing additional skills that can enhance your performance and contribution for you to be recognized. Below are the most relevant skills that you need to acquire so that you can accomplish your goals.

Developing Your Cognitive Mind To Think Like A Winner

Cognitive psychologists have studied the conscious and unconscious mind for many decades and have revealed that the conscious/cognitive mind is the only thing in the world that you have total control of. They describe the "sense of control" in which you have in your mind as the foundation of great achievement and total happiness.

Psychologists have gone on to reveal that your level of peace of mind, mental well-being, and quality of interactions with people is directly correlated with the degree of control that you have for your mind. Taking control of your cognitive mind and training it to think like a winner especially in difficult circumstances will aid you in achieving all your goals.

Your aim should be to study winners across various fields and train your mind to think like those people. You want to instill in your mind the positive values you learn from successful people and then completely believe that you can be a winner just like them and that nothing will stop you from achieving your goals.

Developing Resilience

If resilience can be visualized as a physical object, a rubber ball would be the perfect object that truly captures the essence of resilience. When you throw a rubber ball against a hard surface, it will bounce back. In the same case, resilience is the ability to bounce back when faced with adversity.

If you throw a rubber ball across an empty field, it will travel a long distance. But if you put obstacles in the field, it will not go as far. Resilience works in the same way. Unfortunately, life is not an empty field. There are countless obstacles you need to get through, but resilience will give you the strength to cope with obstacles so that you will be able to achieve your goals and come back stronger from them.

Commitment To Achieving Your Goals

Commitment is the exact opposite of safety, simplicity, and comfort. It is about being dedicated and motivated to achieve goals. The question that you must ask yourself is, does your level of commitment match your goals? To truly develop as a person and realize your dreams, your level of commitment toward your goals must supersede the tranquility of comfort and simplicity in your life.

Commitment is the fuel that pushes us to take action toward reaching our goals. It is the willingness to take up responsibilities and challenges and power in order to succeed in life. Commitment is essential in becoming a winner. It involves setting aside luxuries and distractions, rolling up your sleeves, and doing what it takes to finish tasks.

Surrounding Yourself With Positive People

We are constantly surrounded by a variety of people in our daily lives that influence us in different ways. People tend to pick up the behaviors and tendencies of the people they surround themselves with both consciously and subconsciously.

Were you aware that people emit energy waves wherever they go? People often say that moods and feelings are contagious. In most cases, if the mood of the person next to you is negative, they will radiate the same negative energy/mood toward you and vice versa. So how does one distinguish positive from negative people? The following questions will help you distinguish them:

- Do they inspire/motivate you?
- Do they support you or empower you?
- Do they make you happy?
- Do they make you feel bad or put you down?
- Do they make you feel drained after spending time with them?
- Do they use you for their selfish gain?

Positivity and negativity can mean different things to different people, but once you've answered these questions about the people you surround yourself with, you will be in a better position in determining if they are influential to you or not.

In short, positive people inspire or motivate you to become just as productive as them. They support and empower you with the tools and resources you need to pursue your goals. They will rarely distract you from your objectives but will celebrate and cheer for you when you meet your goals.

On the other hand, negative people are parasites that embed themselves in your life and try to monopolize your time and resources. Such people tend to come into your life to suck off all of your energy and happiness. They like to play the victim and will prey on your soft spot so that you'll do things that will only benefit them. They also tend to make you feel guilty if things don't go their way.

Chapter 13. More Than Motivated: Mindset Changes You Need to Make

The Trouble with Motivation

Do you frequently find yourself saying things like, 'Oh, if only I had to willpower to do X!' or, 'I wish I felt motivated to do Y!' and wonder why you never get anything done? If this sounds like you, then you urgently need to re-evaluate your thinking around motivation.

Motivation is a glorious state of mind. When you feel motivated, you want to take on the world and cross items and goals from your to-do list. Your mind feels sharp, and your energy can seem limitless. Your goals and values seem perfectly aligned, and in extreme cases you can feel unstoppable, particularly if you are an emotionally volatile individual.

So, what's the problem with using motivation as a primary driver for working towards your goals? Well, in brief, such states rarely go on for long. The classic example of this phenomenon is the person who resolves that they will start attending the gym and lose weight. They may even make this their New Year's Resolution, telling everyone that this will be the year they finally get slim and healthy.

We all know how this story ends. What usually happens in this scenario? The person in question may go to the gym for a few weeks and may change their diet for a little while, but soon their old habits come creeping back. Their motivation drops when they don't see the fast results they hoped for and when they realize that the whole project is a lot more work than they had imagined. Suddenly they can devise multiple excuses as to why they cannot go to the gym or cook healthy meals. The whole project suddenly feels very tedious, a kind of self-punishment, and the costs in terms of time and effort quickly start to outweigh the rewards.

The above example illustrates the problem with relying on motivation – it waxes and wanes. Typically, we feel excited and motivated about a project or goal when things are going in our favor, when everything seems to be easy. It doesn't take much time or effort to latch onto an aspiration or dream – the dream of a fitter body or a larger paycheck, for example – and become excited. It's when the harsh reality kicks in and we realize that we need to actually do some work does our motivation wane. This is why you cannot rely on it in place of self-discipline. Motivation is like a fairweather friend; there when the going is good, but flaky when things get hard. Self-discipline is more like a stalwart companion or even a firm but loving parent – perhaps they aren't quite as 'fun,' but

Another problem with running on motivation is that normal life events readily get in the way of even your strongest intentions, and before you know it you start struggling to even keep sight of your goals. For example, to continue with the weight loss example above, let's suppose you vowed to attend the gym three times a week every week starting from January. Let's say that the first couple of weeks go well, and you are fired up by your own enthusiasm. You feel very motivated. Everything is going great.

However, then the inevitable happens – life throws you a curve ball. One evening you might have to stay late at the office, and then tell yourself that you are too tired to work out. Or perhaps you get into a fight with your partner or spouse over the weekend, and the final thing you feel like doing on a Monday morning is your scheduled workout. Suddenly, motivation doesn't seem enough to keep you going any more. At this point, most people give up on their goals and backslide into their way of life.

What's the solution? How can you avoid being at the mercy of your feckless motivation? The answer is to cultivate self-discipline and use that as your life philosophy and general approach, rather than looking to unstable, elusive feelings of motivation to fuel you in pursuing your goals.

The Change You Must Make: A New Mindset

From this day forward, you are no longer the kind of person who waits to feel a sense of motivation before they work on their projects, their goals, or their lives. You need to recast motivation from a necessity, something you feel as though you absolutely 'need' in order to get you through the day, to a nice 'bonus feeling' – a pleasant extra buzz that can give you the edge, but one that you never depend upon. Instead, you will be working to build a set of healthy mental habits that mean you'll never have to 'motivate yourself' again.

A Virtuous Cycle

This may seem strange and even uncomfortable at first. The notion of having to 'show up' and get things done however they may feel on a particular day is almost abhorrent to most people! But this is the harsh reality – it doesn't matter how you actually feel when you are undertaking a particular task. What matters when it comes to achieving your goals and making your dreams come true is simply that it gets done. It is much more effective to finish a project with a grimace on your face than it is to only complete part of it before running out of drive or 'steam.'

But here's the funny thing. When you truly make a shift in your thinking, relying on self-discipline and good lifestyle habits rather than fleeting and unreliable feelings of motivation, you will begin to feel more driven than ever before. Why? Basically, you get caught up in a positive cycle of maintaining a positive attitude, which allows you to succeed in whatever you choose to do, which in turn provides you with some encouraging feedback, which in turn helps you maintain a positive attitude...and so on.

So how exactly do you formulate a solid framework of self-discipline? By adopting a new set of mental tools and habits that act as a springboard for success. To start with, you need to learn the psychology of pleasure and pain. Turn the page to see how.

Conclusion

A person who does not read is as good as a person who cannot read. Likewise, knowledge without action is pointless. One cannot accomplish success, glory, and prosperity simply by reading about it and feeling motivated. You have to go out there and put it into practice to get stellar results! Don't ask if something really works. Ask if you have it in you to make it work. You have to sweat it out and give it your all to emerge victoriously—whether it is working harder on your goals or giving up a bad habit.

To build self-discipline, you need to build grit by:

- Having a sense of purpose
- Working on daily goals
- Practice becoming better and keep the company of gritty people
- You need to be mentally tough, which comes from gaining emotional stability, better perspective of things, and combating daily stress.

You also need to improve your focus, which you can do by overcoming the urge to multitask, taking breaks, looking at red and green objects, drinking caffeine and getting enough sleep.

Finally, to boost your productivity, reduce the number of daily meetings, apply the 80/20 rule, eliminate time wasters, gauge how much time you spend on different activities, stop overthinking, and delegate or outsource when possible.

If you really want to succeed in life, you need to have an unstoppable sense of self-discipline to guide your actions. Without it, you will only keep coming back to your old self – unsuccessful and unwilling to change for the better. In this volume, we have conferred the importance of having a well-renowned discipline and how it can affect our values towards success. Self-discipline is the foundation of all actions towards a person's dream. It guides one's confidence, vision, goals, emotions, and behavior. It governs and defines whether a person will and can accomplish his goals for the future. It allows a person to obtain helpful habits and morning rituals that can help a person to stay productive despite the trials in life.

Self-discipline is your weapon against temptation and other forms of enticement. It pushes you to break your cycle that has been holding you back from starting on the road to success. We also mentioned that lazy days are inevitable, but with a strong sense of self-discipline, you can find yourself on your desk, ready to accomplish your tasks for the day.

Never neglect to have confidence, commitment, and persistence. All of these help you build unstoppable self-discipline that can change your life for the better. Not only will self-discipline push you to your limits and learn from your experiences, but it can also help you overcome your fears into becoming the next big thing! The power to control your mind easily lies in your willingness to thrive against all the odds and grab every opportunity you can to experience. Nobody can live your life better than you do. No one can control your mind and behavior as much as you. Never disregard the power of self-discipline towards your success because it will always serve as your fuel and your drive to a fully transformed self.